Uptime

Uptime

Strategies for Excellence in Maintenance Management

John Dixon Campbell

Productivity Press
Portland, Oregon

Productivity, Inc.
P.O. Box 13390
Portland, OR 97213-0390
United States of America
Telephone: (503) 235-0600
Telefax: (503) 235-0909
E-mail: info@productivityinc.com

Cover design by Bill Stanton
Typeset by Laser Words (Madras, India) and ETP (Portland, Oregon)
Printed and bound by Edwards Brothers in the United States of America

Library of Congress Cataloging-in-Publication Data

Campbell, John Dixon.
    Uptime : strategies for excellence in maintenance management /
John Dixon Campbell.
        p.   cm.
    Includes bibliographical references and index.
    ISBN 1-56327-053-6
    1. Plant maintenance—Management.   2. Total productive
maintenance—Management.   I. Title.
TS192.C36   1995
658.2′02—dc20   94-27005
                                                                  CIP

05 04 03 02 01 00   11 10 9 8 7 6

Contents

Publisher's Message

Since the first English-language book on total productive maintenance was published in 1988, manufacturers have become increasingly aware of the central role equipment management plays in improving production values like output, quality, delivery times, and especially cost. Today, more and more companies are striving to achieve lean production processes. As a result, strategies that can reduce costs while assuring and even increasing equipment capacity and capability are now being considered in boardrooms as well as in maintenance divisions. Why? Because, while maintenance is just one portion of the asset life cycle, it is an important one. Maintenance costs can constitute anywhere from 3 to 50 percent of production costs. Getting the most out of equipment during its productive life with a minimum investment is thus a serious business goal. And in *Uptime*, author John Campbell reviews the most effective elements in the design of a world class maintenance management program from a much-needed business manager's perspective.

Understand that maintenance is more than a *cost* of doing business. World class equipment management is a *way* of doing business that begins with paradigm shifts in thinking and planning at the top and changes the way everyone in the company works with and thinks about equipment. An equipment-focused strategy can emerge only when business planners know precisely the strengths and weaknesses of the company's current maintenance management systems and the actual condition and performance levels of critical production equipment. The strategy results from:

- Projecting current conditions against the backdrop of world class achievements in equipment management
- Quantifying the value of achieving those goals for the company
- Making a realistic investment in support of the new systems, activities, and roles that will accomplish them.

Parts I and II in *Uptime* on Leadership and Control will help the business manager comprehend this important process.

Understand also that an equipment-focused strategy promotes change in two directions at once:

- Raising the levels of equipment performance dramatically
- Changing the relationship between people and equipment and changing the supporting information systems in ways that will assure continuous performance at those higher levels.

The first direction emphasizes reliability improvement as the premiere cost-reduction strategy. Success in this area requires a thorough understanding of continuous equipment and process improvement—the priorities, principles, and methodologies required. The second direction aims to maximize maintenance efficiency and effectiveness by involving people in new ways and using new measures and methods of measurement to enhance and assure control. Both areas are addressed in detail in *Uptime*'s Part III—Continuous Improvement, in its chapters on reliability centered maintenance and total productive maintenance.

We extend our thanks to the Productivity Press staff and other individuals who helped create this book: Diane Asay, project management and developmental editing; Karen Jones and Mary Junewick, editorial management; Marianne L'Abbate, copyediting; Vivina Ree, proofreading; Carol Brookhyser, index; Bill Stanton and Susan Swanson, design and production management; Bill Stanton, cover design; and Laser Words and Electronic Technical Publishing for graphics and page composition.

Norman Bodek
Chairman

Connie Dyer
Director of TPM Research and Development
Productivity, Inc.

Acknowledgments

This book actually started in the maintenance office at the Ford Saline plant in Michigan in 1989. During a discussion about TPM with some of the supervisors, I sketched a pyramid model of the basic building blocks for effective maintenance. These blocks now form the chapters of this book.

There are many clients and colleagues who have influenced *Uptime*: Ray Pomroy at Lever, Toronto; Robert Moore at HEC in Tasmania; Juan Francisco Martinez S. at HYLSA in Monterrey, Mexico; Terry Palmer at Hamersley Iron in Perth, Australia; Alan Gordon at Molson's in Canada; Dan Goehler at Chase Brass in Ohio; Connie Dyer of Productivity, Inc. in Portland, Oregon; and Mike Knowles, Brian Hurding and many other colleagues at Coopers & Lybrand. Special thanks to Andrew Tausz, who provided much needed crafting to my style and engineering lexicon, and to Diane Asay and her team at Productivity Press in Portland.

Finally, this book is dedicated to my wife and personal cheerleader, Beverly, who managed the chaos around me while I wrote.

John Dixon Campbell
Toronto, 1994

Introduction

We all know how much rests on our physical and financial well-being. Personal and professional happiness depend greatly on how well we take care of business. Good health, your own or your company's, depends on keeping all your parts in proper working order. So it's surprising that so many organizations neglect one of the essential elements of success. In most companies, business suffers because we don't pay enough attention to maintenance.

What do we gain by maintaining our physical assets with the same care as our human and financial resources? First and foremost, we gain *Uptime* — the capacity to produce and provide goods and services. Also, we expand our process capability, or the ability to produce goods and services to the customer's satisfaction, consistently. Finally, more than ever, we can predictably provide a safe and controlled work or service environment, with a minimum of risk.

Many senior executives and managers are surprised at the total cost of maintenance. Though it varies directly with the capital intensity of the business, maintenance can be as much as half of production costs (see Figure 1). The numbers in Figure 1 do not include the sales value of lost production, nor the cost associated with rework, rejected product, or recycled materials.

For managers concerned with the end result — what is produced — and how to sell it, maintenance can seem

Sector	Percentage
Mining	20 to 50
Primary metal	15 to 25
Manufacturing	5 to 15
Processing	3 to 15
Fabrication and assembly	3 to 5

**Figure 1. Ratio of Direct Maintenance Cost
to Total Value-Added Costs**

inconsequential, a matter of tweaking here, tightening there. But keeping a company's inner workings primed is a complex job. The kind of detailed work involved doesn't come cheaply. Several key concerns impact the cost of asset maintenance. Some of them are difficult, indeed, to quantify:

- How do we attract and keep capable people to maintain sophisticated equipment systems?
- What is the optimum level of inventory of maintenance parts, materials, and consumables?
- Do we need specialist maintenance engineering support?
- What organization arrangements are appropriate?
- How much and what should we contract out?

Although these questions are not new, today's global competitive stakes make it more important than ever to get the answers right. Business is under enormous pressure to be financially productive. Everywhere, the dictum is the same — maximize output of goods and services and minimize input of resources — financial, human, and physical. Provide the best value to both the customer and the shareholder, but at the same time be environmentally conscious.

Providing value clearly has to do with giving the best quality, at the least price. To satisfy customers, an enterprise must respond quickly to service goods throughout their life cycle. It follows, then:

$$\text{Value} = \frac{\text{Quality} \times \text{Service}}{\text{Cost} \times \text{Time} \times \text{Risk}}$$

The higher the quality and service for a given cost and response time, the more value to the customer. So the physical resources employed—equipment, fleets, facilities or plants—must be available when needed, and must produce at the required rate and quality, all at reasonable cost. Environmental and safety risks must be minimized.

World class enterprises are responding to this value equation. Their quest is not only to reduce costs, but variation and cycle time as well. Likewise, expectations for asset performance have increased dramatically.

New manufacturing and processing philosophies and cost-effective designs of capital equipment have spawned matching maintenance responses. In this book, we'll examine these concepts and tactics and how they've been put into practice. Numerous industries are working to gain competitive edge with some of the most innovative approaches in maintenance management:

Total Productive Maintenance—developed in the Japanese automotive sector, particularly Toyota and its related companies, now spreading to high-precision and process industries

Reliability Centered Maintenance—civil and military aviation, with the introduction of wide-bodied aircraft

Terotechnology—proposed by the British Departments of Industry and the Environment

Logistics Engineering—various military defense sectors, to enhance readiness

Computerized Maintenance Management Systems—most medium and large enterprises, to manage equipment, material, labour and cost data

Expert Systems—particularly diagnostics for fleets, and managing complex equipment systems in the process industry

Condition-Based Monitoring—notably for rotating equipment, high temperature environments and lubricants

Contract Maintenance—in larger process operations and heavy industry, particularly for plant shutdowns and turnarounds

Each of these concepts and tactics can add significant value, increasing asset effectiveness and reliability. But none is the whole solution to boost productivity. Unfortunately, many enterprises embrace one new approach as if it alone were the answer to a complex and highly integrated business process — maintenance management.

Maintenance management is important to all business sectors — and critical to those that are capital intensive. As its importance becomes better understood by management at large, the ability of an enterprise to provide customer value will increase.

Uptime is a discussion of some of the latest thinking and practices for maintenance management, from a business perspective. It is intended more for the general manager than as a definitive technical review of plant engineering and maintenance technology.

Uptime is structured in four parts: beginning with effective Leadership, then gaining Control of the maintenance functions,

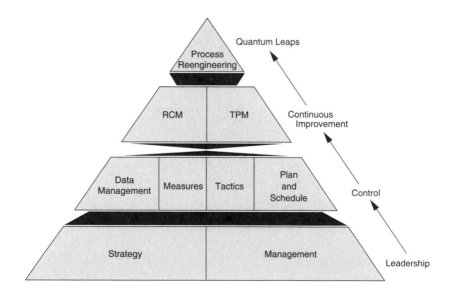

Figure 2. World Class Maintenance

advancing to Continuous Improvement activities, which set the stage for Quantum Leaps in asset productivity. Figure 2 is a graphic depiction of this structured approach which serves as a framework for the book.

Part I, Chapter 1 describes how to create a practical vision for maintenance by developing an asset strategy, effectively integrated into the enterprise's business plan. Human resource management issues for maintenance are then discussed in Chapter 2, with an emphasis on the management of change, so necessary when moving to a culture of continuous or radical improvement.

In Part II, the process and procedural aspects are described to help ensure equipment life-cycle productivity. This section includes chapters on planning and scheduling; the level of maintenance that should be carried out according to value and risk; types of performance measures; and finally, information management.

I have then grouped two of the more successful methods for continuous improvement in Part III—one a logical, disciplined, and engineered approach called reliability centered maintenance (RCM); the other based on employee involvement and total quality principles, called total productive maintenance (TPM).

Finally, the last part deals with the emerging paradigm of achieving radical breakthrough improvements by reengineering the basic maintenance processes. I have used a building-block pyramid metaphor, to stress the necessity of solid foundations before soaring for the stars. Nevertheless, I want to encourage you throughout to look up, and aim high.

Part I

LEADERSHIP

1
Building a Maintenance Strategy

"When you get to a fork in the road, take it."
Yogi Berra

If you were to go to your corner service station and ask the owner-mechanic if he knows who his key customers are, he would tell you right away. He deals with them directly every day. He understands their needs; he's made it his business to know. His livelihood depends on it.

In larger enterprises, such as manufacturing and processing plants, most employees and specialist managers don't know their customers or understand their real needs. This crucial information is left to the sales staff or marketing department. They, in turn, pass along what they learn to the corporate development department. There a company strategic plan is fashioned and eventually makes its way for approval to the executive floor. In this compartmentalized approach to business management, putting together a maintenance management strategy linked to the company's overall business plan can be daunting, to say the least.

Keep in mind that what works for maintenance is not much different than for the business generally. You have to know where you are, how well you are doing, and where you are going. A typical business strategy has the following elements:

- A description of the current products and services, and of the key customers and their degree of satisfaction.
- An analysis of the financial performance.
- A review of the competitive environment and state of the marketplace.
- The strengths, weaknesses, and key competitive dimensions of the business.
- A description of the business vision in, say, five years.
- A statement of the mission, guiding principles, and major objectives to be accomplished and the business plan to achieve them.

Once the company defines and communicates its business strategy, the same approach can be applied to maintenance.

MAINTENANCE MANAGEMENT IN CONTEXT

Going back to basics is the first step. Think about the job that maintenance is meant to do.

Simply stated, maintenance keeps an asset performing to the standard that is required. Maintenance management deals with the planning, organizing, and controlling it takes to accomplish that. But many questions remain unanswered:

- Can we design for better maintainability?
- Can operating procedures affect asset performance?
- How does maintenance impact asset life-cycle costs?

Clearly, maintenance is only part of the asset life cycle. It covers the time when the productive capacity needs of, for example, a vehicle, press, or pump are set to its disposal. Maintenance is one step in a nine-step asset management process, described in Figure 1-1.

We are so programmed to think and act in functional silos — "I design, you operate, and someone else fixes" — that we often miss the overall business process. We're cheating ourselves of the insights that others in the organization could

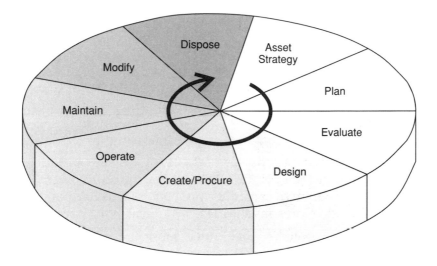

Figure 1-1. Optimizing Life-Cycle Investment Value

contribute. The more input that is provided, the easier it is to understand the need for an asset, design it to meet customers' requirements, build it so that it performs precisely and consistently, and maintain it easily and inexpensively.

Asset management begins by asking why the asset is required and how it relates to the business plan. After that, a closer look sets the purpose, function, and standards of performance. It is then justified, comparing costs to benefits, and ranked as an investment option by the company. After approval, detailed design and specifications are completed. The asset is constructed, or procured, and installed. Once it gets a thumbs-up in testing, it is operated and maintained (and often modified as time goes on). When the asset's economic usefulness is ended, it is disposed of.

Reaping the cost-benefits of an asset rests on all nine steps. Ideally, maintenance, operations, engineering, materials, accounting, and any other relevant department will be involved each step of the way.

FRAMEWORK FOR THE STRATEGY

Building a maintenance strategy follows the model described in Figure 1-2. Foremost in any business plan are the needs and wants of the customers, shareholders, and other stakeholders. The key objectives for each function and element in the business strategy are drafted with them in mind.

Maintenance is likely to have the following targets:

- Maximize the production rate of a particular product.
- Phase out the operation of a plant or product line.
- Add productive capability (assets) for another plant.
- Eliminate stores inventories through vendor partnering.

Clearly, it wouldn't make much sense to carry on maintenance as usual if the plant were to be closed partway through the year.

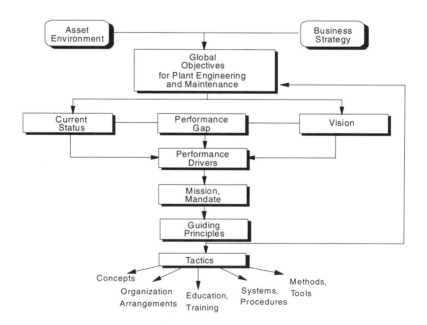

Figure 1-2. Maintenance Strategy Model

A maintenance strategy is like any other tool of business —
it is not meant to hammer away in only one direction. If the
company's situation changes, so must the maintenance model.

One organization restructured so radically that every job
was altered. Former employees could apply for the fewer
positions that resulted. The "new" maintenance engineering
manager set key three-year objectives:

1. To re-engineer the entire maintenance management
   process, with particular emphasis on preventive and
   planned corrective work.
2. To set the terms for, select, and implement a computerized maintenance and inventory management system.
3. To introduce a multi-skilling pilot project in conjunction
   with the union local.
4. To augment the short-, medium-, and long-range maintenance planning capabilities.

These four objectives were the foundation of the maintenance vision. They would ultimately shape the annual plans
and budgets of the department. The first step in realizing these
goals was to take stock of the current situation.

THE MAINTENANCE DIAGNOSTIC

Maintenance improvement fails when there's little understanding of the situation at hand. There may be a strong incli-
nation in the department to retain the status quo, or there could
be friction between production and maintenance. Technically, it
may boil down to lack of knowledge about automation or how
to predict probable failures.

Say, for instance, a trucking company wanted to use
CAD/CAM rebuild technology to build a world's best practice
for engine overhaul. That goal would fail if the trucking firm
hadn't established a solid, systematic maintenance program
first — one that is appropriate for its own business strategy.

Before embarking on an improvement program, assess thoroughly the strengths and weaknesses of the present system and which areas should head the list for enhancements. Your diagnostic must be a clear roadmap of the next step to achieve the vision. It should be comprehensive and cover strategic, procedural, technical, administrative, and cultural issues.

Appendix A is the table of contents of a maintenance management diagnostic review. Major areas of this review are:

- Business characteristics.
- Maintenance environment and strategy.
- Organization arrangements and human resource management.
- Maintenance administration.
- Planning, scheduling, and work order management.
- Preventive and predictive maintenance (tactics).
- Equipment records and histories.
- Purchasing, storage, and parts inventory control.
- Performance measurement and customer satisfaction.
- Automation and information technology.

Another way to perform assessment is to distribute a self-administered questionnaire. Participants are asked to rate various aspects of plant engineering and maintenance. Instead of an independent specialist reviewing, for example, the maintenance environment and asset management, participants would be questioned about the kind of approach in place — whether it's a three-year improvement plan, annual budgeting process, or maintaining equipment on an ad hoc basis.

Each response is scored and plotted either on a histogram (Figure 1-3) or on a Bell-Mason type spider diagram (Figure 1-4). In Figure 1-3, this example has ten categories. The areas requiring the greatest attention are performance monitoring and reporting, and the work order system. In Figure 1-4, this company has done quite well in the categories of planning and scheduling, and materials management.

Finally, maintenance management is perceived differently throughout an organization. Production, engineering, senior

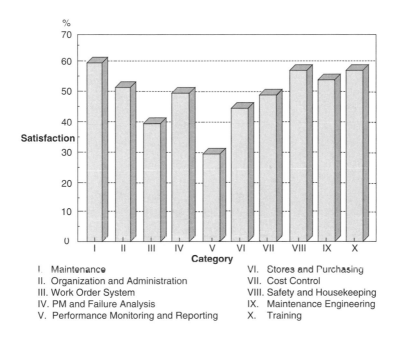

I.   Maintenance
II. Organization and Administration
III. Work Order System
IV. PM and Failure Analysis
V.   Performance Monitoring and Reporting

VI.   Stores and Purchasing
VII. Cost Control
VIII. Safety and Housekeeping
IX.   Maintenance Engineering
X.   Training

Figure 1-3. Self-Evaluation of Maintenance Management Summary Results

management, an area or trades grouping — all have their own needs. A simple grid, measuring nine broad areas against the current status, can give a qualitative score, from Innocence to Excellence. Figure 1-5 provides an example.

Comparing the perceptions of one department to another can be quite revealing. At one base metal extrusion plant, four groups evaluated the status of their maintenance function. Production, maintenance, and front office management all scored their status at approximately the Competence level. Project engineering, however, rated it well below, at Awareness. When the results were discussed with all groups together, it was clear that project engineering was remote from day-to-day activities. This assessment not only shed light on a new strategy for maintenance, it highlighted the need for project engineering to become more involved on the shop floor.

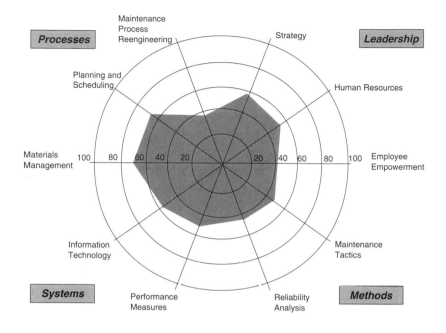

Figure 1-4. Maintenance Self-Assessment Results

DEVELOPING THE VISION

Once you understand where maintenance management stands, a shared vision must be developed. *The difference between the current reality and the vision is, in essence, your maintenance improvement plan.*

This vision may be somewhat nebulous at first. It will emerge, however, if the strategic model is followed. Again, your main goals must be based on the overall business plan, and the major differences between "best practice" and current reality must be understood. Two steps remain:

- Ensuring "best practice" is a realistic vision for your industry sector and your particular operation.
- Setting priorities for the various factors assessed.

MAINTENANCE EXCELLENCE GRID

	Strategy	Human Resources Management	Planning & Scheduling	Maintenance Tactics	Performance Measures	Information Technology	Employee Involvement	Reliability Analysis	Process Analysis
Excellence	Set corporate maintenance strategy/asset strategy.	Multi-skilled independent trades.	Long-term and major project planning and engineering.	All tactics employee-based on analysis.	Equipment effectiveness; benchmarking; full cost database.	Fully integrated; common database.	Autonomous work teams.	Full value-risk program.	Regular review of process cost, time, quality.
Competence	Long-term improvement plan.	Some multi-skilling.	Good job planning, scheduling, engineering support.	Some CBM; some PM; few surprises.	MTBF/MTTR availability; separate maintenance costs.	Fully functional; linked to financials/materials	Continuous improvement teams.	Some FMECA applied.	Some review of administration, engineering and trades procedures.
Understanding	Annual improvement plan.	Decentralized mixed trades groups.	Planning group established; ad hoc engineering.	Time and use based inspections; some NDT.	Downtime by cause; maintenance cost available.	Fully functional; no link to other systems.	Formal workplace improvement committees.	Good failure database; well used.	Some reviews of trades processes, tactics.
Awareness	PM improvement plan.	Partly centralized for some trades.	Troubleshooting support; inspection scheduling.	Time-based inspections.	Some downtime records, maintenance costs not segregated.	Basic maintenance scheduling; some parts records.	Some improvement, safety meetings.	Collect the data; little used.	A one-time review of maintenance process.
Innocence	Mostly reactive to breakdowns.	Highly centralized.	No planning; little scheduling; no engineering.	Annual shutdown inspections only.	No systematic approach; maintenance costs not available.	Manual or ad hoc specialty systems.	Only union-staff mandated meetings.	No failure records.	Never reviewed

Figure 1-5. Maintenance "Innocence-to-Excellence" Evaluation

Benchmarking is an excellent way to start. This technique, discussed more fully in Chapter 5, involves looking at how the leaders in the field achieve your own performance targets. Included could be a sister plant within your organization, a successful competitor, an enterprise somewhat related to what you do, or simply an operation that performs the benchmarked process better than anyone else, regardless of its industrial sector.

Obtaining this information may be difficult, especially from a direct competitor. A published review of maintenance engineering may be the best option. Technology and management periodicals and newsletters often publish features on innovation and best practice.

Understand your own strengths and weaknesses before studying how others manage maintenance. When it does come time to compare notes with other operations, be sure to have a list of specifics — the statistics and how they get their results.

There is a significant difference between stating a vision and having all concerned accept it. Those who will be responsible for achieving the vision should be involved in the maintenance plan. An excellent way to do this is to bring them together for an off-site strategic planning session. Try building team decision-making with, for example, brainstorming and nominal group technique or prioritization matrices. Giving them the chance to help create the plan will encourage the participants to pull together. They'll feel responsible for making it work.

Someone to facilitate this group session should have no direct stake in the outcome. That way, you'll get objective leadership and more individual involvement. Of course, that person must have some knowledge of modern maintenance management methods to extend the reach of the vision.

CLOSING THE GAP — PLANNING IMPLEMENTATION

With the maintenance review and vision determined, you must devise a plan for achieving the vision. Consider:

- The task and its key activities. For example, Planning and Scheduling includes identification, prioritization, materials, labor/skills, worksteps, safety considerations, justification, approval, production scheduling, capacity planning, execution, reporting, followup, and customer satisfaction.
- The priority of the initiative, relative to others. If you have several improvement projects, how much senior management time will each receive?
- Estimated resources and level of effort required.
- The "champion," or person responsible for ensuring successful completion, and the "sponsor" to provide the resources.
- The start date, completion date, and milestones along the way.
- The goal to be achieved on successful completion, and what you're going to measure to determine if you're on the right track.

One business with a solid history of reliability and profitability developed an overall physical asset management strategy, which dealt with most of the asset management process described in Figure 1-2 and included companywide objectives for fixed asset accounting, economic evaluation of projects, and maintenance management. Because of the high average age of their assets, there was an increasing demand for refurbishment, in an environment of cost reduction. A key division developed its maintenance strategy based on this companywide one.

- *The Mission* — "To maintain assets to meet customers' needs cost effectively; to continuously improve skills and processes to optimize asset life, using best-fit methods and technologies; to work safely and be environmentally responsible." Each word was crafted after tedious but heartfelt debate by those who had to live by it.

- *Objectives* — A vision was set by looking at their current situation — their challenges in structure, planning, methods, skills, applied technologies, and measures — and by agreeing what was possible over a three-year horizon. Five long-term objectives were selected to fill the gaps between the reality and vision. The focus was on having higher equipment effectiveness than the industry average at a lower maintenance cost based on the replacement value of assets employed.
- *Action* — Each objective was "owned" by a champion, who committed resources, developed a timetable, and structured a detailed implementation plan. Orchestration of these plans was key to overall success. They held bimonthly progress review meetings to share successes and manage frustrations.

CONTRACT MAINTENANCE

Contracting maintenance activities is strategically important. Most businesses contract out some form of maintenance, whether specialized technical work, like nondestructive testing, or overflow fabrication and machining work. In North America, about 15 percent of maintenance is subcontracted to a third party; in Japan and Europe, it is about double that.

Contracting maintenance has many benefits, not the least of which are labor leveling for shutdowns and cost and capability factors. It does have some drawbacks, such as the difficulty in controlling quality and getting the labor experience needed. To answer the strategic question of whether you should consider contracting significant portions of your planned and preventive maintenance, you have to understand first the concept of competitive advantage. Your business has one or several core products and services provided to its customers. To produce these, there are a few core processes and physical assets that allow these processes to happen. Does — or could — your cost effectiveness and capabilities in maintaining these assets be considered a competitive advantage, something that allows you to compete and win in the marketplace? If so, by contracting out maintenance of these assets, you may be giving away some of your competitive advantage.

If, for strategic reasons, you plan to contract maintenance, your key concerns will be around contractor productivity. Ideally, the contractors will be subject to a thorough review, appropriately trained, and not subject to high turnover. You should try to contract specific, well-defined projects or responsibilities and ensure that performance standards are set and monitored closely. There should be clear lines drawn between in-house and contract involvement. Contracting can bring a lot of flexibility to your business, but it requires assertive management and control.

Despite a clear strategy, the best-laid plans can go astray. You'll greatly minimize the chance of that happening if you follow the lead of the mechanic at the beginning of this chapter—know your customers, then dedicate yourself to satisfying their needs.

2
Managing Change

"Change is not what it used to be."
Charles Handy
The Age of Unreason

Next to death and taxes, change is one thing you can always count on. Today, change is faster than ever, and it is unpredictable. Many businesses are left scrambling, uncertain how to catch up.

Such a charged atmosphere demands quick reflexes to remain competitive. In the past, an outside expert was often brought into an organization to research and design changes. This was followed by an edict from executive management to put these ideas into practice. History teaches us that this dogmatic approach tends to produce mixed, short-term results, at best. What's needed today is change from within. An organization must steer its own course in an organized and controlled fashion toward a predetermined goal or vision.

Change can be described as a movement from one state to another, through various transitional forms, to a final condition. For plant engineering and maintenance, the main objective is to boost equipment productivity. This can involve many areas, each of which is in a state of flux:

- Increasingly complex technology in every aspect of work.
- Integrated information and data management for employees, fixed assets, costs, performance, and activities.

- Advancing process automation and robotics requiring less operators and more highly trained technicians.
- Tighter design tolerances for higher quality products and less maintenance intervention.
- Shorter obsolescence cycles as time-to-market for new products decreases.
- Larger scale of plant with increasing flexibility.
- Higher investment targets and profit margins in the new global economy.
- More rigorous health and safety standards in all jurisdictions.
- Raised environmental expectations by both regulators and consumers.
- Increased degree of contracting as businesses stick with their core competencies and contract out the rest.
- Product liability law changes.
- Workers' expectations for self-realization in their jobs.

In Chapter 1, a strategic direction—or vision—for maintenance was described. To be successful, this vision must be embraced by every employee at all levels. They must understand, accept, and, particularly, internalize the need for change.

An organization can be altered only by the individuals involved. In short, to change requires a compelling need and a shared vision. It also requires the means. An overall approach to organizational and job change is summarized in Figure 2-1.

The most difficult aspect of change is usually convincing those concerned of the need to change. That's not easy, especially when it means destabilizing the entire organization. The impetus for organizationwide change is often the threat of business closure or a protracted strike by the employees.

There are several more positive approaches to try. An independent review of maintenance management or overall asset management can be an appropriate starting point. An outsider's objectivity and logical insights are invaluable. A customer satisfaction survey can provide information on how the organization is perceived by its clients. (Area maintenance listens to production, repair shops listen to area maintenance, etc.)

1.   Establish the need to change.
2.   Get all employees involved and committed.
3.   Set the objectives.
4.   Define the approach.
5.   Clarify the boundaries.
6.   Collect all the facts and analyze.
7.   Prepare options and select the solution.
8.   Develop the plan.
9.   Carry out the plan.
10.   Measure and communicate the results.

Figure 2-1. Overall Approach for Change Management

This destabilizing basically means shaking up the status quo — in turn, freeing up employees to think of better alternatives and thereby allowing the organization to move. Ideally, change should make the organization more effective, and, at the same time, make work more interesting and satisfying. Employees must not only endorse the new methods, they must play a large part in designing them. If they're not involved, the situation will not improve and the organization could be harmed.

People resist change for many reasons. Fear is chief among them — fear of the unknown, of losing skills and status, and of not being able to cope. Some employees may see it as implied criticism; others may criticize those introducing the change or the need for change itself. Still others may not agree with the targeted end result, especially if they've had little or no input or if the new plan appears to be foisted on them from outside.

It helps to understand what psychologists refer to as the "cycle of loss" (see Figure 2-2) when introducing significant change in people's lives. The cycle of loss was developed to counsel people when they have experienced a major setback — the death of a loved one, divorce, or bankruptcy, for instance. It also applies when a major change occurs in our working lives.

At first we deny that there is a need for change, such as the contracting out of much of what we thought was our core

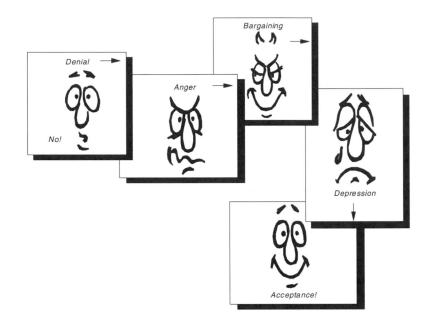

Figure 2-2. Reactions to Radical Change

work. Then comes anger that this should happen, followed by bargaining to cure the symptom, not the root cause. Depression follows with full realization. Finally, there is acceptance of the new reality. Understanding this cycle of loss can help us cope with change and manage the way it is introduced.

Figure 2-3 depicts the change process as a force field. Change occurs when there is an imbalance between the sum of restraining and driving forces. When a steering group, study team, or task force is inaugurated, consider conducting a force field analysis. Document the key drivers and restraints to change in the organization.

There are three basic strategies for achieving change:

1. Increase the driving forces.
2. Decrease the restraining forces.
3. A combination of 1 and 2.

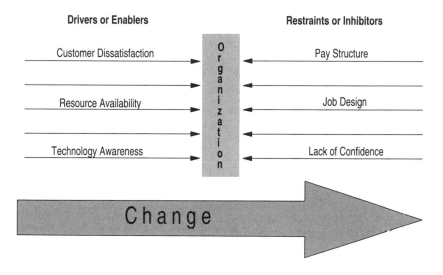

Figure 2-3. Force Field Analysis Example

By providing information through education and training, you will greatly improve the odds for success. Instead of being directed from the top, employees will participate in the make-over and have time to get used to it.

The benchmarking of indicators, processes, and organization structures can also help determine both the direction and rate of change, particularly if the organizations studied are best in their field. Some noteworthy attributes of change in successful companies are that:

- It was directed strategically.
- It was participatory.
- The team approach was used.
- It was balanced in functions.
- It was flexible.
- It was integrated (not simply interfaced).
- There was excellent communication.

Leadership style is key to implementing change. If leaders are not fully committed—if they vacillate, subtly or overtly question the need, or have more pressing priorities — success will be severely diminished. If leaders, wanting to encourage participation appear aloof, the team will question the importance of what it's doing. On the other hand, if leaders dominate the change process with a personal vision, others can resent it and become inflexible. Leadership is a fine balance of providing commitment, motivation, and direction.

In short, change is more acceptable when:

- It is understood.
- People affected have helped to create it.
- It has been planned.
- People can share its benefits.
- It does not threaten security.
- It results from previously established principles, rather than personal edict.
- It is effectively led.

The most obvious implication of any significant change in an organization is the structure itself.

ORGANIZING THE MAINTENANCE STRUCTURE

Maintenance management became an important topic in the 1950s and 1960s. Large-scale, complex, automated factories and process facilities became prevalent. Consumer demand pushed these factories to near-capacity. Uptime was paramount, and control was key.

Maintenance organizations were centralized through the maintenance manager. This person was responsible typically for all aspects of plant and facility support: mechanical and electrical trades, electrical power, steam, compressed air and water services, maintenance engineering and planning, repair shops and custodial work, and grounds and civil maintenance. Almost all services were dispatched centrally, and all spares and materials were regulated from the main or central stores.

The strength of this system was twofold. It ensured control over policy, procedures, systems, quality, and training. Second, efficient leveling of the workload across the operation was guaranteed. The major disadvantage was inflexibility, which was felt in many ways:

- Sluggish response time to production requests.
- Tradespeoples' ignorance of specific equipment in the plant.
- Customer unawareness of the trades.
- Rigidity in approach, procedures, and policies.
- High chargeout rates to the local areas and bureaucratic processes.
- Customer dissatisfaction over allocation of resources.
- Strict demarcation among the trades, and between maintenance and production, creating "turf wars."
- Focus on efficiency, not effectiveness.

Global competition and the push for long-term profits transformed centralized management theory. Production became the responsibility of area or product managers, who had to react quickly as economic conditions changed. Also, management participation and job enrichment for front line workers began to improve productivity and effectiveness. This has fueled decentralization and moved maintenance into the mainstream of operations.

Despite its popularity, decentralization is not a panacea. Some crucial questions remain. Does central control always lead to inflexibility? How are risk management and maintenance engineering handled consistently from department to department, under full decentralization?

What's clear is that a dogmatic approach does little to balance unique technical, systems and behavioral complexities. A better approach is to revise the maintenance strategy — its mandate, policies, key objectives, and structure. It is important not to lose sight of the enterprise business plan and the environment in which the maintenance function must perform.

There is no correct organization structure that can be transferred from a book to a real-life situation. There are only strategies to be effectively applied in specific situations. Usually the best solution to organization restructuring for maintenance is a hybrid of centralized and local area functions.

The 2-million-square-foot plant of a microelectronics operation in the midwest of the United States was divided into four focused factories producing different products: chemicals and components, connectors, hybrid electronic circuits, and capacitors. After the introduction of the just-in-time manufacturing philosophy, these focused factories were further divided into sixty production cells. The maintenance had been centrally dispatched to the various cells, but this arrangement was causing unacceptably long response times and less than satisfactory customer service. It was rare to have the same maintenance technician dispatched to the same cell on different days, so the learning curve for the technician exacerbated the delay. After much soul searching and debate among maintenance and production managers, it was agreed to have the following structure for maintenance:

- Central maintenance for facility maintenance (HVAC, etc.), stores inventory warehousing and control, fabrication and machine shops, tooling, information database control, and specialized trades training.
- Focused factory maintenance for workshops, planning and scheduling, operator training in maintenance, and maintenance engineering.
- Cell maintenance for multi-skilled teams (sometimes covering several cells), urgent maintenance, preventive maintenance, and consumable and free issue parts and supplies.

It's always important to keep in mind the ultimate objective of the maintenance function — to provide effective equipment at a reasonable cost — when you're looking at structure.

MULTI-SKILLING

We can see that, as decentralization and flexibility took hold, it became essential to improve labor skills planning and scheduling. Managers had to offset the inevitable duplications in a decentralized system with higher asset performance and labor productivity. One option was to train workers in multiple skills.

There were several other challenges at the time that multi-skilling was introduced: boundary disputes and communication difficulties, workload leveling, demands for job enrichment, and general management career path planning. In response, organizations started contracting out to smooth workload peaks. They set up centralized floating trades teams for shutdowns and major overhauls. Also, maintenance and production duties were shared, increasing the know-how of the decentralized maintenance team.

Multi-skilling means providing employees with all the skills necessary to do their tasks effectively. Through job enrichment, it promotes individual initiative. The aim of multi-skilling is flexibility. Its objective is not to have everyone do everything and eliminate specialist skills or loosen standards for quality work. If multi-skilling is approached simply to slash costs rather than improve productivity, its most significant long-term benefits will be lost.

It isn't surprising that organized labor has some legitimate concerns about multi-skilling:

- There is normally no marketable, generally recognized skill certification that can be transferred to other organizations or jurisdictions. Multi-skilling programs lock in employees.
- Training programs can be poorly conceived or inadequate.
- Multi-skilling ignores traditional career patterns, where long or valuable specialist experience leads to promotions into management.

- Some organizations generalize skills to meet management's immediate needs, again reducing mobility.
- Multi-skilling could be a precursor to contract maintenance.
- Often, organizations introduce multi-skilling programs with staff reductions and inappropriate compensation schemes.

These issues must be addressed and discussed openly early in the process to foster employee involvement and commitment.

Planning for multi-skilling should center around a training needs and task analysis. What tasks are currently being carried out and by which trades? Is the current skill level appropriate? What are the most frequently performed tasks of some typical jobs or work orders?

This information can be found in work order histories, industrial engineering studies, and maintenance manuals, or through employee questionnaires and surveys. Figure 2-4 shows an example of the relationship between various trades and some of the tasks performed.

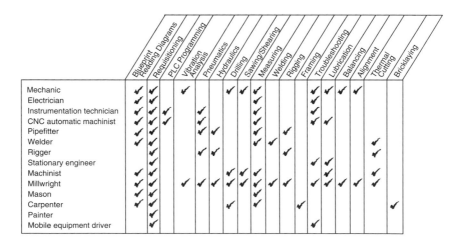

Figure 2-4. Trades-Tasks Relationship

Through the task and needs analysis, you can develop an overall education and training approach. Many organizations discover that more basic education is necessary before skill training can start. The first priority may be upgrading employees' literacy and facility with numbers. Then they may benefit from a clear description of the company's markets, customers, products, services, and overall strategy for success. Other general information could include basic computer skills, statistics, and modern concepts and methods in maintenance management and quality management. Try alternating classroom and on-the-job experience, including job rotation. The results of the needs analysis will, of course, set the agenda.

It may help to put the many tasks performed by maintenance into skill modules. Clusters of these modules are then linked for logical multi-skilled groupings and progression.

Multi-skill training should not be attempted without considering compensation. Employee representatives in many cases help design pay-for-knowledge systems, in which workers are paid for learning new skills. They must, of course, use the skill when and where it is needed. Make sure you can measure the output, then reward improved performance and teamwork with bonuses and other benefits.

Multi-skilling pays off, but at a price. To the direct cost of increased compensation, add significant investment in training and facilities, management time, and changes to existing systems. The company will also pay, at least initially, for some of the time taken for training — either directly or through a larger workforce.

Nevertheless, the long-term benefits of multi-skilling are worth the sacrifices. You can expect:

- Increased flexibility in scheduling workers.
- Shorter response time.
- Reduced need for supervision.
- Greater labor and asset productivity.
- Higher morale among workers.
- Improved scheduling, communication, and integration.

- More stable employment.
- Greater job satisfaction.

Following is a case study showing how one consumer goods company, Lever, fared with a multi-skilling program. Lever, a Unilever company, manufacturers soaps, detergents, and other laundry and personal hygiene products. They operate several plants in the United States and Canada, one of which is located in Toronto. After the signing of the North American Free Trade Agreement (NAFTA) between the United States and Canada, the competition for the rights to manufacture various products was heightened among the Lever plants. The Toronto plant increased the productivity and flexibility of its maintenance workforce through multi-skilling. The overall objectives were:

- Broaden the scope of skills for each tradesperson.
- Reduce the complexity of trades demarcation.
- Provide new career paths.
- Increase the skill level of key trades.

The philosophy was "one-job — one person."

Working closely with two community colleges, Lever designed a series of courses to enable, say, a millwright to acquire basic electrical skills, and an electrician to become skilled at alignment and vibration. A career progression was developed so that millwrights and electricians could achieve a supertrade category, earning skill-based incremental pay as they progressed. Figure 2-5 summarizes the training modules required for the multi-skilled and super-skilled trades at Lever.

During the first round of training, about 80 percent of the trades participated in upgrading or expanding their skills, with 95 percent of these eventually passing their courses. Each person has a record of the various modules completed and those remaining to achieve the next level. This multi-skilling process is ongoing, with discussion between management and the local Teamsters union.

The provincial government has now approved the trade of "multi-skilled industrial mechanic," with the requisite skills

Module/Skill	Millwright/Industrial Mechanic	Packing Mechanic	Electricians	Instrumentation	Supertrade
1. Safety	✓	✓	✓	✓	✓
2. Communications	✓	✓	✓	✓	✓
3. Trade science	✓	✓	✓	✓	✓
4. Blueprints	✓	✓	✓	✓	✓
5. Hand and power tools	✓	✓	✓	✓	✓
6. Machine tools	✓	✓	✓	✓	✓
7. Measurement	✓	✓	✓	✓	✓
8. Fasteners	✓	✓	✓		✓
9. Lubricants	✓	✓		✓	✓
10. Rigging	✓				✓
11. Materials handling	✓	✓		✓	✓
12. Power transmission	✓	✓	✓	✓	✓
13. Compressors & Pumps	✓	✓			✓
14. Prime movers	✓	✓	✓	✓	✓
15. Weld, braze, solder	✓	✓	✓	✓	✓
16. Bearings, seals, packing	✓				✓
17. Valves, piping	✓			✓	✓
18. Fans & blowers	✓				✓
19. Electrical controls	✓	✓	✓	✓	✓
20. Pneumatics	✓	✓		✓	✓
21. Hydraulic	✓	✓	✓	✓	✓
22. Predictive maintenance	✓	✓	✓	✓	✓
23. Milling, grinding	✓	✓			✓
24. Lathe work		✓			✓
25. Packing machines		✓			✓
26. Electrical circuits		✓	✓	✓	✓
27. Electronic systems		✓	✓	✓	✓
28. Electric power distribution			✓		✓
29. Programmable logic controllers			✓		✓
30. Drive systems			✓		✓
31. Microprocessors			✓		✓
32. Process equipment				✓	✓
33. Process control systems				✓	✓

Figure 2-5. Multi-skilled Trades at Lever (Toronto)

and training requirements. This recognition increases the marketability of participants. Lever and the union are working toward the development of a super multi-skilled technician, with expanded troubleshooting and technical training skills. Multi-skilling has been a major factor in the decentralization of the Toronto plant's maintenance organization structure. Now the multi-skilled trades are an integral part of the area operation teams.

LEARNING, TRAINING, AND DEVELOPMENT

Learning is an attitude, an approach to life. Those who value knowledge don't hesitate to investigate if they suspect there is a more productive way of completing a task. If they find their solution is indeed better, they adopt the practice and let others know about it.

While this makes obvious business sense, there are still variations in companies' performance. Productivity can vary greatly from one plant to another, even after discounting factors such as size, age, and environment. Even in large plants, an innovative practice adopted skillfully by one department can be ignored by another. Common inconsistencies occur in integrating operations and maintenance, cross-training or multi-skilling tradespeople, and empowering supervisors. Making employees, whether they're staff or paid on a contract basis, responsible for productivity and profits will not necessarily produce the results you want.

Finding the most productive methods has a great deal to do with your access to information of several kinds. It depends on the attitude, knowledge, and skills of the employees. It means sharing ideas and innovations. And it requires an open pipeline to the best practices in other similar industries.

In *The Age of Unreason*, Handy describes the learning process as a wheel divided into four parts. It starts with a *question*, or problem to be solved. Then it moves on to *speculation* or theory. Next comes *testing* the theory, and finally, *reflection*. The learning wheel runs on the "lubricants" of self-responsibility, perspective, and forgiveness. A well-oiled attitude includes accepting ownership for the future, being able to view events from many angles, and being capable of living with uncertainty and mistakes.

Employee education and training is the starting point for fostering a learning environment. This strategy should have:

- A clear objective.
- A review of the training needs.
- An understanding of the unique work culture.
- An implementation plan addressing the training needs and work culture.
- The associated costs and benefits.
- Continual assessment of whether the objectives are being met.

Training can range from basic literacy—so employees can at least read the employee suggestion form—to the latest methods of managing technical people, and just about everything in between. (See Figure 2-6).

What is the exact difference between education and training? And why are both needed to perform technical tasks? A simple example explains. We all would probably agree that our teenage children need some form of sex education. A more debatable subject, however, is their need for training in the area.

The objective of education is to expand knowledge of a topic, to bring an uninformed individual through stages of awareness to understanding. The aim of training is to upgrade a person's skills to do the job effectively.

To define education and training needs, you match tasks with the skills required to execute them. Taking a bottom-up approach—basing plant and equipment maintenance requirements on the manufacturers' recommendations and equipment history records—can be overwhelming.

Instead, if you look at it from the top down—reviewing plant and equipment performance against requirements or expectations—you're more likely to see thorny areas. Many of these problems are caused by gaps in knowledge or skills.

When planning a training program, give thought not only to *what* should be included, but also to:

- *Who*—to optimize the costs and impact on the available workforce.

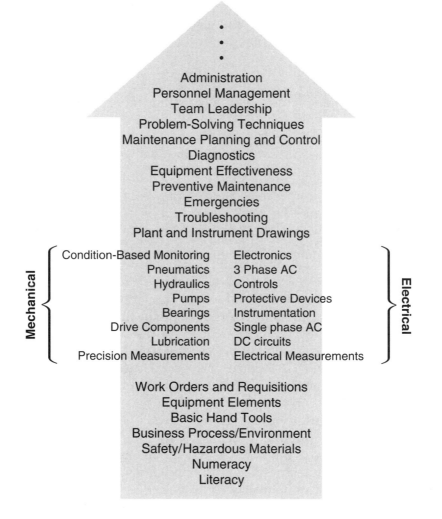

Figure 2-6. Scope of Training Requirements

- *When* — consider plant schedules, cultural issues, after hours.
- *Where* — on-site, off-site, at home, out-of-town.
- *By whom* — community college, supervisors, vendors, consultants.

- *How* — mix of classroom and on-the-job, lecture, audio-visual, home study.
- *How much* — standards, evaluations and certifications.

Managing others is as essential a skill as expertise in crafts or trades. Too often, though, no thought is given to training people how to manage. The typical first line supervisor is promoted for being technically adept and a team player. He or she may not have any inherent ability to manage.

A maintenance manager with no understanding of leadership, administration, budgeting, and productivity control can be a liability. Most people are not born leaders. They must be taught.

Many planners act solely as parts chasers, clerks, or data entry personnel. Because they have little shop floor experience, their credibility can be seriously questioned by the trades and supervisors.

For people to learn to handle change, they need education. They also need encouragement. Sharing positive results is the best way of ensuring more of the same. Not only will the public recognition motivate others, it will expand everybody's knowledge. An open exchange of ideas, leading to increased productivity, is what you're trying to accomplish.

COMPENSATION AND REWARDS

The best way to attract qualified, enthusiastic technical employees is to reward them generously for their extra efforts. If you don't pay any more or provide other benefits, few will want the more demanding, higher risk jobs. The prospect of a major commitment to education and training will pale without a direct payoff, even though increased skills can bring long-term rewards.

Your compensation program should depend on your organization's overall objectives as well as your maintenance strategy. One or more approaches may be appropriate.

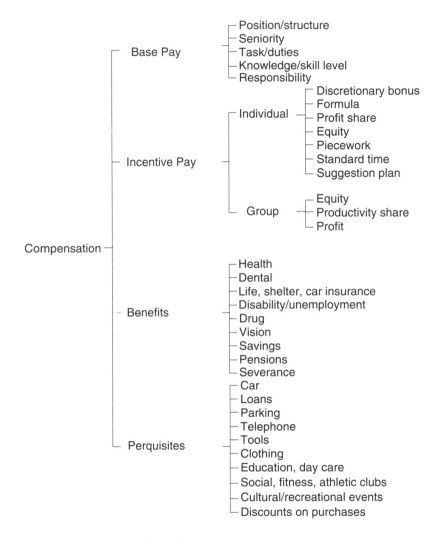

Figure 2-7. Compensation Categories

Figure 2-7 divides compensation into four main categories: base pay, incentive pay, benefits, and perquisites.

- *Base pay*—In any compensation system, base pay must be competitive and guaranteed. The technical trades employed in maintenance work are in great demand. If you want low turnover, begin with an appropriate base pay. It is normally related to an employee's position, grade, or seniority, and the tasks or duties required in the job description. But in the case of multi-skilling, it should be based on the knowledge or skill level demonstrated by the employee.

- *Incentive pay* — Incentive schemes can be designed around either individuals or groups. With the exception perhaps of suggestion plans, the trend is away from individual incentives, particularly with engineered standards, toward group productivity gain-sharing plans. These plans are used to reinforce desirable team behavior and employee involvement. Productivity gains are shared between the company and the employees, according to a predetermined schedule.
- *Benefits* — Traditionally, benefits have encompassed both the social safety net and basic life and disability insurance. In many jurisdictions, some of the basics, such as unemployment insurance and pensions, are legislated. More recently, with increased pressures to cut costs and share decision-making with employees, some enterprises are offering a menu of benefits. Each is priced so employees can select the most appropriate cluster of benefits up to a preset dollar limit.
- *Perquisites* — Perks are popular when the economy is expanding and competition for highly qualified employees is keen. In maintenance management, the most common perks are subsidized personal work tools and equipment, education leave, and financial assistance.

Nonmonetary rewards are another way, besides base and incentive pay, to recognize individuals and groups for a job well done. There is usually no set pattern for perks, which vary greatly depending on the organization. Most began perks as thanks for achievements in throughput, safety, or project management or for completing formal training courses. Now, they've been extended for significant contributions in quality, service, cost and time improvements, and for advances in job-based knowledge or competence. Awards can range from certificates, medals, and trophies, to dinners and get-away weekends.

Today's trend in compensation is away from strict trade limits to demonstrated knowledge and skills. It also shows that management is sharing the company's financial success with employees and recognizing their career aspirations.

We started this chapter looking at the extent of change in the marketplace and the need to respond quickly and effectively. Handling change really boils down to managing people well. Doing that is not only something you teach, it's a life-long learning process. Your own workplace version of the three R's — reassess, recognize, and reward — will earn you top marks for your efforts. Best of all, you'll make change work for you.

Part II

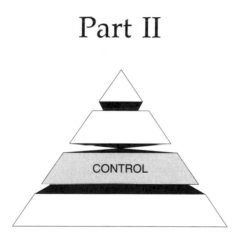

3
Planning and Scheduling Resources

"The surest way to be late is to have plenty of time."
Leo Kennedy

What every plant or fleet manager wants most is to sleep soundly — to turn off the office light at night confident that the equipment will be running reliably and efficiently the next morning. Unfortunately, such peace of mind is rare. Breakdowns, emergency repairs, unplanned and unscheduled downtime, overtime, maintenance stores stockouts — all rob your business of capacity and profits.

What you need is a maintenance program that is effectively planned and scheduled to reduce labor and downtime when something goes amiss. Ensure that the correct parts and materials are used and your repair will be of higher quality than an unplanned one. Here's what it takes:

- A sequenced, documented plan is made, with descriptions and drawings of what has to be done. Take time to review the repair manuals. Use the most highly skilled people, rather than whoever is available, or whoever will stay on overtime.
- The job isn't started until all the right parts are on-site.
- It is scheduled for the best production window with the least disruption to customers.

45

Studies done by several research teams, including Alcan and General Motors, have shown a clear link between planned maintenance and reduced costs. Not only does it make intuitive sense, it's statistically sound. Not every running repair, of course, needs detailed planning and scheduling. But it is clear that jobs involving complex procedures, specialist skills, and replacement components and parts certainly do.

THE SIX KEY STEPS

Effective maintenance work comes down to six key steps. The process starts with identifying what has to be done and ends with analyzing why you had to do it in the first place (see Figure 3-1).

Identify

The need for maintenance work can spring from something as simple as a noisy bearing or something as complex as interpreting trends in vibration signatures. Random observations have a low probability of catching a problem before it becomes expensive. It is much better to program inspections by operators who are equipment sensitive.

Figure 3-1. The Maintenance Process

Like your family car, your equipment will benefit from regular cleaning, lubrication, adjustment, and observation for signs of abnormal performance. These are important checkpoints for early signs of problems. And they can help you decide where in the "repair queue" a job might be positioned.

Plan

Planning is ensuring that all the resources necessary to do the job are accounted for. Scheduling is a matter of when to do it. The most obvious planning tasks are to determine what has to be done, in what sequence, and with what skills. Parts, materials, and components are usually necessary and often not immediately at hand. Sometimes, extraordinary items or resources are needed, including engineering drawings, outside contractors, special tools, or mobile equipment. Safety reminders or regulatory direction may also be required.

The planner, of course, must be someone who has the technical skills and plant-specific experience to be credible to those executing the plan. The planner may be able to take advantage of standards to help lay out the job and estimate how long it will take. Finally, estimate the overall cost, allowing cash flow projections and repair-or-replace decisions.

Schedule

In the final analysis, scheduling is a matter of availability. When can you coordinate with the people who have the needed skills? Do you have the parts? Do you have the agreement of the production department to release the equipment?

To schedule the skilled people, you need to look first of all at who's at work, then who is sick, on vacation, or on a training course. There are also mandatory jobs that will, or should, have priority. These include preventive maintenance, the normal load of emergency work, and other planned work already started.

Parts availability is a matter of checking the on-hand status of the maintenance stores or the lead-time of any items ordered directly from suppliers. In many cases there is a credibility gap between what the stock records indicate and what is actually there. Visual confirmation is highly recommended until you gain confidence in your store keepers and their inventory control system. For equipment scheduling, you will need a close working relationship with both the production planners and shop-floor leaders.

Assign

The assignment of the job depends on the organization arrangements in place. Autonomous, self-directed work teams do all but the most specialized maintenance diagnostics and repair work themselves. More traditional organizations usually delegate the day-to-day work assignment to the area or craft foreperson. In either case, it is usually helpful if the team or foreperson has a few days of planned work in advance. This allows for flexibility, as emergencies, unplanned work, or crew changes fluctuate.

Execute

This is where 'the rubber hits the road.' Well-trained, motivated team players keep the maintenance process revolving. They add the real value—quality, cost, time, and service. If the maintenance team is supported by effective systems, treated fairly, and allowed to proceed with the work, you'll be rewarded with cost-effective maintenance management.

Analyze

The job isn't finished until the paperwork is done. Thoughtful analysis of the failure, and your response to it, will lessen the chance of repeating the same mistakes.

At the very least, the maintenance work should be incorporated into the equipment history. Especially if the work was significant, you should redesign the preventive maintenance and operating procedures so the failure doesn't recur.

This is the core maintenance management process. Many enterprises, however, seem to be programmed to hit only the *Execute* button. Firefighting is certainly exciting, and people feel tremendous accomplishment when the fire is put out. But this method of managing maintenance leaves less and less time for sober thought and careful planning. People get hooked on the adrenaline rush while the fire rages — and the "dragonslayer" status of getting it under control. We need to see this kind of behavior for what it is. Praise should be given to the fire preventers and counseling to those addicted to crises.

PLANNING HORIZONS

Issuing a work order to repair a faulty circuit breaker is clearly a different undertaking than maintaining the civically-run power scheme that supplies it with electricity; yet both are related. All types of fixed assets — from a switch to a power station — require at least three kinds of planning: life cycle and long range plans, annual plan and budget, and work orders and projects (see Figure 3-2).

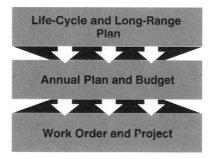

Figure 3-2. Planning Horizons

Life-Cycle and Long-Range Plans

This type of planning is closely associated with strategic planning for maintenance, discussed in Chapter 1. The planning process involves creating a vision of future performance, including human, financial, and physical resources. It also includes action plans to achieve the vision.

Life-cycle planning for the physical plant, equipment, and fleet means getting the most economically from maintenance and operating activities. Age is not the best indicator of failure rate in most complex equipment systems. It is usually helpful to develop a long-range forecast of major project and maintenance costs, based on past experience. Besides studying history, scheduled inspection for age-related maintenance—painting, corrosion work, roads and civil structures, roofing—can help the plan.

These life-cycle plans are geared for major or significant work. They should fit neatly into the operation's overall business strategy. Make hefty expenditures only on assets that contribute long-term value. Keep in mind that any new or replacement capital purchases will have a direct bottom-line impact on maintenance requirements of all kinds.

Annual Plan and Budget

If you don't plan and budget properly, you are jeopardizing all of your efforts to improve maintenance quality. Empowering workers and integrating the department with production, for instance, won't really pay off if the equipment isn't adequately maintained and enhanced.

What's needed in the annual maintenance budget and plan is clearcut—accurate equipment histories, periodic inspection, condition-based monitoring, and emphasis on continuous improvement. Plant shutdowns, equipment overhauls, and major inspections should be forecast by month, priced, and incorporated. New technology, systems, and procedures, and organization changes that affect capability, must be factored in.

This type of zero-based budgeting and planning is more challenging than relying on last year's budget, plus or minus 5 percent; but it's far more useful for planning the staff, long lead-time parts and materials, and cash flow. It commits everyone to the concept of planned maintenance throughout the year.

Work Orders and Projects

In recent years, particularly with the advent of just-in-time manufacturing and the advances in microcomputers and software, the maintenance work order has received much bad press. The typical paper-driven work order had anywhere from three to eight copies: the originator, the planner, the supervisor, accounting, the scheduler, production, and the tradesperson. In some operations, a work order number was required for *every* job done by the maintenance department, and for *every* item released by the stores.

There is, however, a happy medium. Let's first examine the use of a work order. It is a:

- Planning and scheduling mechanism for complex jobs.
- Cost collection mechanism for labor, stores requisitions, purchase orders, and services to charge against a piece of equipment or production cost center.
- Way to capture delays and measure productivity.
- Tool to determine and manage work backlogs.
- Means of saving equipment histories to analyze failure and the effectiveness of your preventive maintenance efforts.

The advantages are numerous. Today, there are inexpensive and simple computerized maintenance management software packages available so that the benefits can be enjoyed with little paper.

PLANNING AND SCHEDULING TOOLS

The most effective tool is the computerized maintenance management system. Most commercially available systems have comprehensive modules that include work order management, equipment records and history, preventive maintenance tasks and scheduling, costing and budgeting, materials management, and labor skills capacity planning. Chapter 6 deals exclusively with this tool.

The Gantt Chart

A useful yet simple tool for planning and scheduling is the Gantt chart, first introduced by Henry T. Gantt at the beginning of this century (see Figure 3-3). This technique lists key steps and activities along a vertical line and the time needed to accomplish them along the horizontal. When properly constructed, it gives:

- The sequence of events.
- The duration of each event.
- The start and end times of each event.
- The overall project start and end times.

It is particularly useful for events that are either strictly sequential or are independent. It does not, however, clearly show interdependence among different projects.

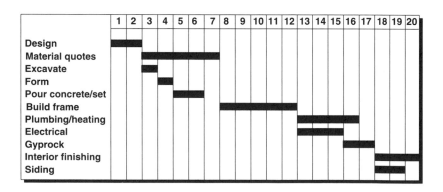

Figure 3-3. A Gantt Chart

The Critical Path Method

To frame a plan that shows relationships between different facets, you could use the critical path method or activity network diagram. It will determine the minimum time required to complete a project, be it independent, sequential, or interrelated.

The time that the activities will take and their best sequence are set out. In building a house, for example, plumbing, electrical and duct work must be completed prior to plasterboard installation and painting. Landscaping, which is independent of interior work, can only follow excavation.

Once plotted, the path with the longest duration is highlighted on the critical path (see Figure 3-4). There are several microcomputer software packages of varying sophistication available to help determine the critical path. They can also plan and schedule the resources necessary to execute the plan.

The Pareto Diagram

One of the simplest yet most powerful tools is the Pareto diagram. Vilfredo Pareto, an Italian economist (1842–1923), came up with the 80-20 rule, that is, 80 percent of the problems are associated with 20 percent of the equipment.

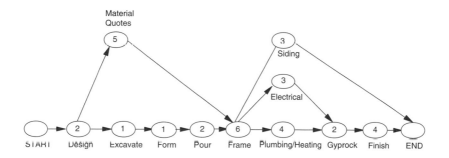

Figure 3-4. A Critical Path

Equipment Type

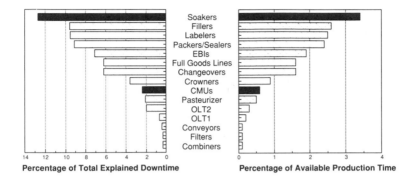

Figure 3-5. Bottle Shop Downtime Histogram

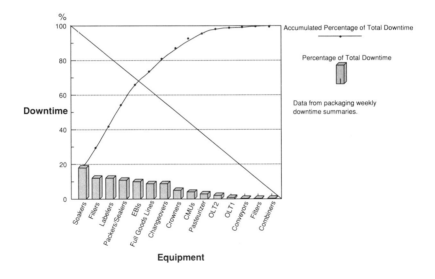

Figure 3-6. Pareto Downtime Analysis

The Pareto diagram is a bar chart used to prioritize, help separate the vital few from the trivial many. In Figures 3-5 and 3-6, the downtime of a bottle-filling shop is analyzed and compared with the available production time. The priority for redeveloping the PM program should be the soaker, rather than the combiners, fillers, or conveyers.

PLANNING STANDARDS

Time standards in maintenance have a negative ring. They conjure up images of a dogmatic, authoritative organization culture. They remind us of the days when techniques such as Universal Maintenance Standards, Methods-Time-Measurement, and Engineered Performance Standards kept employees on a tight leash.

These techniques have little place in today's workplace. If you believe in a team approach to continuous improvement, an environment that truly values the total employee, you'll see no benefit in time standards that measure and control individual productivity. They are attempting to cure a symptom, not the root cause.

That said, we still need to know approximately how long a job will take. We must be able to estimate its cost, schedule it along with other jobs, and determine the equipment downtime needed to complete the work. In a broader sense, we can apply useful standard quality operating and maintenance procedures, as well as benchmarks for equipment performance and cost.

Backlog Time Standards

Two of the most practical methods for estimating how long a job will take are equipment history work-order file times and time-slotting. If records are kept, you can link repairs, overhauls, projects, plant shutdowns, etc., with a series of job or work orders. These are usually filed in numerical sequence. Document on these orders, or in accounting records, the employee hours charged. The average actual time is used as the standard.

If you don't have records, or if the plant or equipment is relatively new, time-slotting may be the best solution. Time-slotting is a simple method that uses comparison. For example,

Slot	Time Range	Plan Time	Actual Average (6-Month Moving Average)
A	0-3	1.5	2.2
B	3-6	4.5	3.8
C	6-12	9.0	9.1
D	12-24	18.0	21.7
E	24-48	36.0	35.4

Figure 3-7. Time-slotting Method

it takes less time to change a tire than the brake pads, and less to change the pads than the master cylinder.

The planner selects several common jobs of varying duration and complexity, then times them from either observation, time cards, or expert opinion of those performing the job. They are grouped into categories and used as benchmarks for similar jobs (see Figure 3-7).

If an average of the actual time taken is kept, that number can be used for the planned time. For example, the jobs slotted in D will likely be of the same repetitive type in that particular area over which the planner has responsibility.

Quality Standards

It seems ironic that, while the quality standards of products and the techniques to produce them are becoming more uniform and precise, the work environment from which it all springs has become less rigid. If you think about it, however, one follows the other in a logical way.

Many successful companies are reinventing themselves into lean, flat organization structures. Their employees operate mostly in autonomous, self-directed work teams. This has freed them up to develop the best processes and procedures to achieve perfect conformance. So it should be with maintenance procedures, particularly repetitive tasks such as preventive care, and tool and die maintenance.

Quality standards aren't a matter of employees having the freedom to do what they want. Rather, excellence results when everyone involved is responsible for developing the delineated best practice and is accountable for carrying it out. Once the best practice is determined, the time standard can be determined using actual time averages or the time-slotting technique.

MANAGING MATERIALS

Spare parts, components, consumables, lubricants, fasteners, and all other maintenance materials account for fully one-half of most companies' maintenance budget. This proportion is rising. As more and more of our industrial equipment and fleets are designed for modular parts replacement, material costs devour an increasing portion of the budget. In many industries, however, this area is neglected. To manage maintenance materials effectively — and save yourself many wasted dollars — begin with the basic processes of purchasing, stores and inventory control (see Figure 3-8).

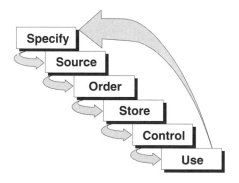

Figure 3-8. The Materials Process

Specify

Specifying what is needed is made much easier if there is an equipment register — an accurate, updated configuration of what you have. Each major equipment assembly or system is then broken down into the smallest component or part that you would buy as a unit. Newer equipment tends to have integrated components that are changed out and returned to the manufacturer for repair or simply discarded. If your records are accurate, the rest of the process will be simplified.

Source

Vendor management used to be a win-lose situation. Confrontations between buyer and seller were the order of the day. Buying strategy dictated that you go for the lowest price of three or more bids for each purchase. One purchasing agent at a public board of education was required by policy to send out a request for proposal for a $2,000 project to all qualified vendors — sixty-three of them!

A much more productive approach is to develop a supplier partnership. You lock in with a trustworthy supplier for one, two, or more years, and work together to try to improve the overall value of the transaction. You gain lower cost, higher quality, and better service. This approach has been highly successful for the North American car industry, helping it compete on a cost, quality, and time-to-market basis with Japanese manufacturers.

Order

Once the specifications and the supplier are known, the part can be ordered. There are two things to consider here. Items kept in an inventory holding account (a balance sheet account as opposed to an income statement account) are normally ordered once the minimum or order point has been reached. The final user isn't involved. The authority to order was established when the order point was approved.

Items not kept in the maintenance stores can be ordered by the user. To simplify, many businesses have only one or two maintenance people placing orders with the buyers to avoid duplication and allow for grouping of requests.

Store

The core job of maintenance stores involves receiving, stocking, and issuing. Numerous factors affect the efficiency of the stores, from its layout to the use of enabling technologies. But one thing that shouldn't be needed, if the source step is done correctly, is a lot of staff inspection for quality and complete order receipts. One company's solution to a 35 percent rejection rate of incoming maintenance supplies was to add receiving inspectors. The problem needs to be fixed at the source.

A direct-order receiving area, for parts ordered by the users from suppliers, is normally a necessary evil. It should, however, be aggressively managed. Otherwise, the part could become obsolete before it's even unwrapped.

Control

Companies normally tie their maintenance stores inventory to the number of active tradespeople they employ. They spend from about $30,000 to $80,000 per person. The prime issue with this investment is its efficiency and productivity. Is it fast moving, turning over at a reasonable rate of, say, twice per year? Or is it mostly for "insurance spares," with one third of the investment still parked (no issues) after 24 months?

Your inventory of spares and materials should be measured and managed rigorously. It deserves the same scrutiny as your raw materials, work-in-process, and finished goods inventory. Although shrinkage is not normally a major issue, free access is not advantageous. It is easy to lose track of what is actually in the stores. Free access should be given only to fast-moving, common items such as fasteners, piping, steel fittings, and the like, and ideally at the workplace where they are used.

Repairables and rotables — components taken out of service, rebuilt, and returned through the inventory control system — are often a contentious issue. There are as many ways of handling this as there are plants with the problem. Usually, it's the cost accounting of repaired components that causes the problem. Free or no-value issue, with a chargeback of the actual repair cost to the last user, is often the easiest way to handle it.

Use

In a recent review of a manufacturing operation, the lag in trades productivity was primarily attributed to waiting for parts. The time taken while a part was looked up, requisitioned, spotted, issued, and brought to the workplace was considerable. Once it arrived, installation was speedy.

Give some thought to "kitting" parts, especially for repetitive work like preventive maintenance or scheduled discard of components. Also, parts delivery to the site may sound expensive, but compared to lost trades productivity and extended equipment downtime, it can be cost-effective.

Analyze the Data

One of the simplest ways to judge the effectiveness of your maintenance planning is to review the number of urgent or emergency requisitions received by the buyers. Another is to check the number of stockouts in the stores, to see if inventory control is working. The objective of maintenance materials management is to balance the investment with the value. Look for ways to continuously improve this ratio.

In this chapter, we've looked at two components that work in tandem to keep your organization moving forward. Without one — proper maintenance planning — you cannot have the other — efficient materials management. A hole in your inventory control can flatten your maintenance productivity. Keep these teams working together to ensure smooth operation.

4

Selecting Maintenance Tactics

"If you want truly to understand something, try to change it."
Kurt Lewin

Armed with the maintenance strategic plan, you are set to do battle against the evils of breakdown. You have the mandate, the strategic objectives, your guiding principles or policies, and a plan for improvement. But when you get right down to the equipment, what are you going to do differently? Actions and their timing are the tactics you need to carry out the strategic maintenance plan and make the difference. In this chapter, we'll look at the tactical options and how to implement them.

TACTICAL OPTIONS

Do you replace your car headlights at regular intervals of, say, six months? Do you wait to replace your tires until they wear through? Or do you check your car engine oil using spectrochemical analysis before replacing it? Each component or system in your car has a function, a most likely failure mechanism, a consequence, and some economic implications. With your headlights, for instance, you let them run to failure, then replace them. After all, you can't tell when they're going to fail, the consequences aren't severe, and they're easy and cheap to replace.

Similarly, you need to know all the maintenance options available for plant equipment and machinery, then decide which ones are the most appropriate. The choices tend to be a blend of both actions and timing.

- *Run-to-failure* — Maintenance is performed only after the equipment fails. This is typical in electronic circuit boards and light bulbs.
- *Redundancy* — Redundancy is built into an equipment system. If the primary unit fails, the secondary unit is available, for example, hydraulic pumps used on aircraft and pumping systems in processing plants.
- *Scheduled component replacement* — At a predetermined point, based on either elapsed time or use, a particular assembly, component, or part is replaced, regardless of its condition. Electric wheel motors in large diesel electric haul trucks are usually replaced on hours operated, for instance, because the repair expense skyrockets if they are run to failure.
- *Scheduled overhaul* — Like the scheduled replacement, the plant or equipment is stripped and overhauled, based on a predetermined plan such as the annual shutdown. This is standard industry practice for petrochemical plants, which take shutdowns every year.
- *Ad hoc maintenance* — Maintenance is done on-the-fly or when there is a production window. Many manufacturers revert to this option when there is a sudden increase in required throughput.
- *Preventive maintenance* — This is based typically on either time or use factors, such as kilometers, cycles, throughput, fuel consumption, and running hours. It is carried out by conducting inspections, cleaning, lubrication, minor adjustments, and other failure prevention actions. Often, records of observed condition are kept for trend analysis. This is typical in processing sectors — food, pulp and paper, minerals, and chemicals — where there are visual signs of wear and corrosion.

- *Condition-based maintenance* — Maintaining plant and equipment is based on its measured condition. Examples include vibration, temperature, stress, contamination, flow, electrical measure, and visual inspection.
- *Redesign* — Designing out maintenance is done particularly for critical equipment where it is difficult to measure the condition or detect imminent failure. A good example of this is your family car. In the 1940s, sedans had a practical speed limit of about 60 km/h. The roads were rough and the cars often had loose nuts and bolts, marginal suspension systems, and inefficient power trains. Engine oil had to be checked frequently, along with the cable controlled braking system. Today, the top speeds are whatever you can get away with, the car bodies are unitized, and the suspensions are robust. The "information center" on the dashboard monitors the condition of everything from the engine to the door locks. Hydraulic disc brakes last longer than the engines did in the 1940s, and the typical maintenance interval is three to six months.

The difficulty comes in selecting the correct maintenance tactic. Which action and schedule is most appropriate when considering costs, plant downtime and risks? From a technical viewpoint, you need to understand how the failure happened and if there was any way you could have prevented it.

Maintenance is usually time-based for a car, but about the only component on a car that will fail strictly on elapsed time is the body finish. It's hard to shake the notion that something is more likely to fail the older and more used it is.

Another common view of age-related failure is what's known as the biological model or the "bathtub curve." This thinking contends that equipment has a greater chance of failing when very "young," followed by a stable period, then is unreliable when very "old."

Recent research into equipment failure probability and advanced age has shown some surprising results. The most significant finding is that there isn't a strong link at all. Another is

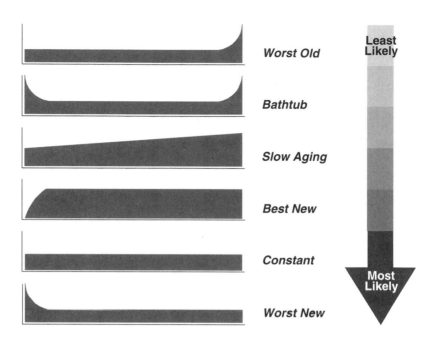

Figure 4-1. Conditional Probability of Failure

that there are six broad relationships, not just one or two. These are shown in Figure 4-1, where time is the base, adjusted for such usage factors as cycles, hours, hours used, and distance covered.

Worst old
- age-related failures
- rapid increase in failures at a particular point of use
- the least common failure mechanism of all
- routine maintenance based on time is effective
- examples include impellers, crusher jaws, tracks, and liners

Bathtub
- high probability of failure at the beginning and end of its life

- two tactics, at least, are necessary to deal with early and end-of-life problems
- it is a combination of "worst new" and " worst old"
- an example is simple electromechanical systems

Slow aging
- steadily increasing probability of failure with age
- associated with corrosion or creep
- usually when equipment is in contact with the product
- use rebuild or component replacement tactics
- pipes, refractories, tires, structural, clutches, for example

Best new
- not age-related, except at beginning of life
- age-based routine maintenance generally ineffective
- as with all random mechanisms, on condition is the best tactic
- hydraulics, pneumatics are examples

Constant
- random failures, not age-related
- complex equipment systems: electronic, electric, mechanical
- routine age-related maintenance is ineffective
- ball bearings are the classic example

Worst new
- most common failure mechanism for complex equipment
- probability declines with age, perhaps because of design, manufacture, construction, or management
- once the infant mortality problem is solved, routine maintenance plays a minor role
- electronics, avionics, highly complex/integrated equipment

This study, therefore, gives us some important tips about how equipment should be maintained:

- Failure isn't usually related directly to age or use.

- Failure isn't easily predicted, so restorative or replacement maintenance based on time or use won't normally help to improve the failure odds.
- Major overhauls can be a bad idea because you end up at a higher failure probability in the most dominant patterns.
- Age-related component replacements may be too costly for the same reason.

Which failure pattern you choose should follow a careful scrutiny of the data. There are subject matter experts around who know your particular equipment. Brainstorming with individuals or groups will pay dividends, whether it involves the experienced operator, the mechanic or electrician, the service representative for the original equipment manufacturer, the area planner, or the clerk who manages the equipment histories. Also, try sampling studies over several months. You'll end up with some useful information, particularly if there are several similar units in operation.

Unless the equipment comes into direct contact with the product or a processed material (like steam or component raw materials in pipes), or unless it is a simple device, age probably will have little impact on whether it fails. Therefore, condition-based maintenance techniques are going to be the most effective.

Knowing the failure pattern doesn't necessarily tell you what maintenance tactic to use. When the steering clutch on a tracked dozer was analyzed, age-related failure patterns were found. But an economic study revealed that it was actually more cost-effective to allow the clutch to run to failure than replace it, despite good prospects of predicting a PM replacement schedule because the failure pattern was age-related.

CONDITION-BASED MAINTENANCE

Condition-based maintenance is usually most effective because it almost always can warn of a failure before it occurs (see Figure 4-2). The warning may be subtle and give you little time

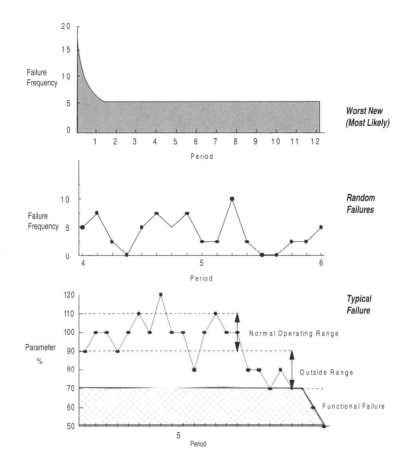

Figure 4-2. Condition Monitoring

to react. When it's obvious, however, you'll have plenty of opportunity to intervene without affecting the equipment greatly.

Key equipment with components that fail in a progressive
manner, rather than without warning, are good candidates for
condition monitoring. Typical components that benefit are large
rotating units. Those components that do not benefit include
integrated electronic circuits, which usually fail suddenly. Selecting the most appropriate method or measurement depends
on several factors:

- The failure mechanism itself.
- The reliability of the method chosen.
- The warning time it gives.
- The cost, both initial and ongoing.
- The skill level required to monitor and interpret the measure.

You'll have an easier time managing cost and skill level if you can use two or three common methods to monitor critical components of important equipment. To illustrate, most small to medium-sized businesses concentrate on fluid and wear particle monitoring from lubricating and hydraulic fluid systems. They also tend to have some basic methods of vibration analysis and thermography. Obviously, this is dependent on the type of equipment in use — high power, high temperature, high speed, etc.

Vibration

Vibration analysis monitors the mechanical movement of a machine. Based on a regular schedule, you watch for vibration levels outside a predetermined range or baseline. The vibration signal is also used to diagnose the location of the problem. The most common vibration sources are misalignment and imbalance, but the most serious is the imminent failure in a rolling bearing. Defining the problem usually involves looking at the amplitude (how much movement), frequency (how fast), and phase (how a machine is vibrating). Compressors, pumps, turbines, paper machines, and other large rotating equipment are the most common applications.

One simple example of vibration analysis saving time and money involves a brewery. The pasteurizer area had a fixed-time overhaul schedule on the pumps for the 30 units each year. At a cost of five trades-days and $1,200 in parts and materials per pump, this added up to over $60,000 per year and about 75 days with one pump out of service. A fixed time vibration analysis schedule was set. Only one pump per year was targeted for overhaul, at a cost of $2,000 plus the ongoing monitoring cost of an additional $2,000 and 2.5 down days for the one pump.

Lubricants

Lubricant analysis — otherwise known as tribology — involves lubricating oil condition and wear particle count. Physical and chemical analysis of the oil — the viscosity and acidity, for example — are periodically compared to a baseline to check for deterioration. The size and shape, as well as a chemical analysis, of the wear particles can indicate the suitability of the oil, the component that is wearing, and the likely wear mechanism. One railway uses lubricant analysis and an expert system to schedule all of its PM routines, component replacements, and locomotive overhauls.

Temperature

Thermography — mapping the surface temperature using an infrared camera — is useful when it can be related to the condition of the equipment. Corona discharge, hot electrical connections, refractory lining defects, roofing and its insulation, and even inflamed human and animal tissue are prime candidates for this condition-monitoring tool. One example is a typical infrared survey of high-voltage lines, substations, main disconnects, and breakers. Problems such as loose connections, deteriorated splices, cracked insulators, and tarnished or charred connections are detected by temperature rises of between 10° and 100°C.

At its simplest, condition monitoring looks at equipment system performance. Precision or quality of the product produced and its cycle time are observed. Also observed are pressure, temperature, flow, amperage, resistance, voltage, and other factors. These parameters lend themselves to monitoring long-term trends in equipment performance and degradation.

Condition monitoring is cost-effective. Depending on the method, it can be done by a semiskilled operator and often indicates both equipment condition and product quality. The equipment operator using the five senses is, therefore, the most versatile and valuable condition monitor!

There are more than 50 condition-monitoring and non-destructive testing techniques, with more sophisticated ones being developed each year. A discussion of these is beyond the scope of this book. However, for specialized, critical equipment that must be available, reliable, and precise because of safety, environmental, or economic risks, a sophisticated condition-monitoring approach is well worth the research.

PREVENTIVE MAINTENANCE

Preventive maintenance can reduce failures and emergency repairs. It promotes equipment awareness and disciplined inspection. It also works well for simple components that become less reliable as they age. In these cases, failures can be reduced by a logical overhaul or replacement schedule.

The first step, then, in developing a PM program is to classify equipment and key components by failure pattern. They're either age-related or they're not. For those that are not, provide some conditioning monitoring. For those that are age-related:

- Set a standard condition, range, or function.
- Prepare inspection, overhaul, changeout, and adjustment routines and schedules.
- Establish recordkeeping, histories, and trending statistics.
- Organize for analysis and periodic updating, based on the results of the routines and schedules.

THE COST OF THE TACTICS

It is almost irrelevant to discuss the cost of maintenance without considering what you are buying. The job of maintenance is to keep equipment running and to enhance its speed, reliability, and precision. If it is done only in a reactive way, after breakdowns occur, downtime and subsequent repair bills will be high.

When you start using preventive maintenance, even just lubrication and badly worn component changeouts, unexpected failure declines, as do the production losses it causes. A preventive approach will mean more and more shutdowns to inspect, adjust, overhaul, replace, and test. These delays can cost you money in lost production time. At the same time, emergency repairs will taper off dramatically.

At some point, there is a balance between the cost of emergencies and that of proactive maintenance. This relationship is shown in Figure 4-3. A note of caution: earlier, we saw that a great majority of equipment does not benefit from age-related routine maintenance component changeouts and machine overhauls based only on use or elapsed time. Figure 4-3 assumes that proactive maintenance is indeed appropriate and effective at reducing unexpected failures.

To truly be prepared, you need experience, proper data collection and analysis, and a combination of good engineering and teamwork. With all that, you can steadily advance to the

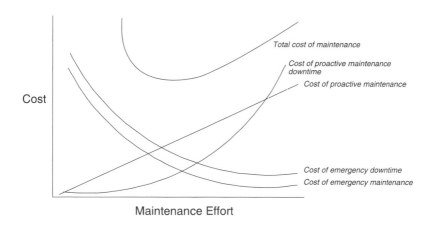

Figure 4-3. Total Cost of Maintenance

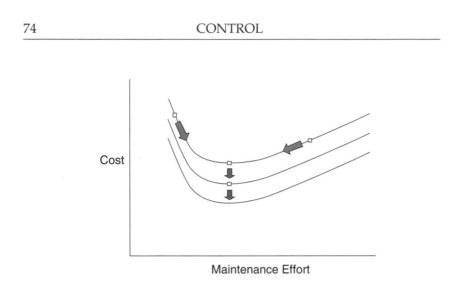

Figure 4-4. Optimizing and Reducing Costs

minimum point in the total-cost-of-maintenance curve. Further, you'll be well-armed to bring the entire curve down, as shown in Figure 4-4.

5
Measuring and Benchmarking Performance

*"People respond to the tools and measures used to evaluate
them and will do the most unusual things to ensure
that they meet their goals."*
Kathleen Leibfried
Benchmarking — A Tool for Continuous Improvement

Management expert Tom Peters said it more briefly: "What
gets measured gets done." But what you measure and how you
do it are critical decisions.

For businesses that run on large, sophisticated equipment
and facilities, maintenance performance has a dramatic impact on
overall capacity and cost. Measuring that performance, though,
is often based solely on the cost of tradespeople and materials, or
it's wading through a muddle of terms like *mechanical availability*
and ratios like maintenance costs over plant replacement value.
Even more useless is tying effectiveness to headcount.

If you want productive maintenance, measure maintenance
productivity. If you want to achieve your maintenance strategy,
constantly review your strategic objectives and master plan. If
you want to be competitive, compare the job you're doing to
others in the field. Learn from your most successful competitors.

MEASURING MAINTENANCE PRODUCTIVITY

Productivity is simply what you get out compared to what
you put in. With maintenance, what you get is better equipment
performance. What you put in is money.

75

Wages, benefits, parts, supplies, facilities, and services all add up. What's needed is a handy, all-encompassing productivity ratio of equipment performance over cost. It doesn't exist, however, at least not in a way that makes any practical sense. Instead, you must break each component down until you have a reasonable set of parameters to judge whether your performance is good, bad, or indifferent.

Equipment Performance Measures

What questions should be asked when measuring equipment performance? Well, the most obvious is whether it's running or not. Then, is it available for use? If it does run, how long would you expect it to keep chugging along before the next failure? What's the average time it would be down for repair and maintenance? How fast can it operate compared to what it was designed for? And how precisely does it run? Does it always produce the quality required? Is its performance improving or deteriorating?

There are commonly accepted terms and definitions to answer each of these performance questions:

- *Availability* — a measure of uptime, as well as the duration of downtime. It is calculated as:

$$\frac{\text{Scheduled time} - \text{All unplanned delays}}{\text{Scheduled time}}$$

- *Reliability* — a measure of the frequency of downtime, or mean time between failures (MTBF). It is determined by:

$$\frac{\text{Total operating time}}{\text{Number of failures}} \quad \text{or}$$

$$\frac{\text{Total operating cycles (km, tons)}}{\text{Number of failures}}$$

- *Maintainability* — a measure of the ability to make equipment available after it has failed, or mean time to repair

(MTTR). It is determined by:

$$\frac{\text{Total downtime from failures}}{\text{Number of failures}}$$

- *Process rate*—a measure of the ability to operate at a standard speed or cycle. This is calculated by:

$$\frac{\text{Ideal cycle time}}{\text{Actual cycle time}}$$

- *Quality rate*—a measure of the ability to produce to a standard product quality, or

$$\frac{\text{Quality product}}{\text{Total product produced}}$$

- *Equipment effectiveness*—an overall measure that considers uptime, speed, and precision. It is measured as a product of

$$\text{Availability} \times \text{Process rate} \times \text{Quality rate}$$

The value of any of these measures has a lot to do with how the equipment was designed and built. Thus, the best test of equipment performance is often its performance trend over time. This will provide you with the feedback or changes in operating and maintenance practices.

Cost Performance Measures

In most businesses, it is difficult to obtain accurate and relevant maintenance cost information. Labor is charged through cost centers and only significant materials expenditures are charged to the equipment. Overhead costs bear little resemblance to reality, since they're allocated based on direct or operating labor.

Accurate maintenance cost information is useful for two reasons. Maintenance productivity can be measured and, therefore, managed. And it promotes rational equipment decisions, such as whether to repair or replace.

Maintenance costs accrue in the following categories:

- *Labor* — all the wages and benefits of the trades and temporary helpers.
- *Materials* — all the supplies, parts, components, repairables, consumables, and other items used by maintenance.
- *Services* — all shops, engineering, facilities, and stores warehousing.
- *Outside services* — all contracted services for HVAC maintenance, specialty services, training, and consultants.
- *Technical support* — supervision, planning, materials coordination, clerical, data entry.
- *Overhead* — other support functions such as accounting, MIS, personnel, and for general utilities, facilities, and other general expenses normally allocated.

It doesn't always help to use maintenance costs in such a generalized way. Instead, you can break them down by:

- Specific areas such as labor, materials, services, and technical support — all of which are influenced by area management and staff.
- Job or work order for labor, materials, and services, so the costs can be designated to a particular piece of equipment.
- Expense type for labor and for material and all services to monitor trends in key parts, consumables, and services.

As with equipment performance, tracking cost trends is more sensible than looking at individual numbers or single averages.

Process Performance Measures

Maintenance management is a business process. The inputs are costs; the output is equipment performance. Between the two comes the complex job of making sure the equipment works at top performance. If the system isn't managed right, no amount of measuring and pressure will help. You need to find the right buttons to push. Here are some suggestions:

- *Emergencies* — If a situation immediately and negatively affects the safety, profitability, or customer value, *and* automatically necessitates overtime, then it is a true emergency. Both the amount and impact of emergency maintenance should be measured.
- *Planned versus unplanned* — There should be very little unplanned work. With accurate equipment histories, recurring repairs, overhauls, and overtime work can be planned for in advance, particularly for critical equipment.
- *Schedule compliance* — A good indicator of the state of firefighting in your plant.
- *PM schedule compliance* — Doing the preventive maintenance activities when they are scheduled is probably the best and quickest way to improve equipment performance.
- *Work orders generated from PMs* — This can tell you a lot about the thoroughness and effectiveness of the PM program. When an inspection is carried out, you should expect some work required some of the time, or the inspection is useless or not done correctly.
- *Urgent versus normal purchase requisitions* — Another test of maintenance planning. If the planning process is working, maintenance knows ahead of time what parts are required.
- *Stores inventory turnover* — Dividing the value of annual issues by the on-hand value of stores says a lot about what is in them. Anything over 2.0 is likely good.
- *Stores stockouts* — Indicates what you are stocking and the service level provided for the investment.

Process performance measurement should be tailored to the unique circumstances of each situation. For example, if cost overruns and poor equipment performance are the effects, what are their root causes? The answer could be excessive overtime, but the reason for it can vary. It could be anything from emergencies that resulted from poor PM compliance to quality problems due to lack of training.

Another way to improve your maintenance performance is to ask your customers. You might find, for instance, that response time is an issue. This affects maintainability and may result from the organization structure (centrally dispatched versus area-based crews, for example). Or the difficulty could be in getting the right parts from the warehouse.

BENCHMARKING MAINTENANCE

Benchmarking is a tool with which an organization compares its internal performance to external standards of excellence — and then acts to close whatever gaps exist. The objective is to achieve and sustain best-in-class performance through continuous improvements.

Contrary to popular belief, benchmarking is not just appraising how your direct competitors measure their performance. Rather, it is looking behind those measures to the practices that produce them. It is about understanding which of those measures and practices are critical to your success, and finding out who performs best, regardless of industry sector.

Consider the case of one mining company that wanted to benchmark its truck engine overhaul practice. It looked first at the critical success factors. Most important, it concluded, were reliability — having long periods between failures — and shop cycle time — reducing the size of the queue and therefore the capital cost.

Then maintenance had its own procedures documented, measured reliability and cycle time, and set about looking for benchmarks. The company's sister mines had similar practices and poorer results; the direct competitors were not much better. Some of the other mining operations in different commodities were improving reliability but through expensive, contracted overhauls by the original equipment manufacturer.

Finally, the mining company discovered an engine rebuild shop with a flawless reputation for reliability, using just-in-time manufacturing techniques to run the shop with remarkable cycle times and short queues. Although it was an airline's jet engine rebuild shop, its planning, scheduling, execution, and control procedures were directly applicable to those at the mine.

As the mining company discovered, you must look beyond your own limitations. It is not enough to improve just incrementally from your past performance or that of other company divisions. To compete globally, you must look everywhere to learn new methods. Make yourself a student of the best of the best, particularly in unrelated business sectors.

The basic philosophy behind benchmarking is:

- Know your own operation, both its strengths and its weaknesses.
- Know those industries that excel at the maintenance processes used in your operation, including competitors, sector leaders, and others.
- Set challenging targets; incorporate the best practices.
- Measure results and strive continually for superior performance.

A European microelectronics company manufacturing computer chips for calculators set for itself what seemed a daunting goal — to improve a production line's reliability from 24 hours to 48 hours within one year. The process could tolerate a few extended production shutdowns but not frequent interruptions, as there were quality losses both at shutdown and at startup. Availability, or the duration of shutdowns, was less significant than how often they occurred, or the reliability factor.

The company thought it faced a tall order   its equipment capability was to be doubled. But when the company benchmarked similar process lines in Japan, it found that reliability there was at 200 hours. The goal of 48 hours was suddenly irrelevant. With that, the company couldn't even attain parity, let alone competitive advantage!

What is benchmarked must be critically important to the customers, the value chain—the factors that affect the organization's success. Not only is the process exhaustive, the improvement plan at the end of it will cost significant time, effort, and resources. Benchmarking maintenance makes sense only if it will bring real gains to the company. Examples of maintenance benchmark processes are shown in Figure 5-1; some measures are shown in Figure 5-2.

Choose the businesses you want to benchmark, keeping several factors in mind. The required information must be

---

Strategy

- Maintenance has a service attitude, with production being the customer.
- Maintenance has an evolving, strategic improvement plan.
- Production and maintenance are seen as partners.
- Ongoing analysis of contractor services ensures competitiveness.
- Focus on business measures of maintenance effectiveness.

Management

- Training needs and programs are matched and evaluated.
- Maintenance teams are decentralized and autonomous.
- Group incentives and individual recognition are in place.
- Performance for everyone is evaluated.
- All employees are involved in maintenance improvement.

Systems

- CMMS is implemented fully and upgraded regularly.
- Maintainers use the system regularly on the shop floor.
- There are no duplicate or private systems.
- Effectiveness and efficiency measures are understood by all.
- New approaches and technologies are reviewed systematically.

Figure 5-1. Examples of Processes to Benchmark

Maintenance	Typical
● Equipment effectiveness	65%
● Availability	95%
● Reliability	45 days
● Emergency response time	10 minutes
● PM schedule compliance	92%
● Supervision:Trades:Support ratio	1:15:2
● Coverage	24 hr/5 day
● Planned/Unplanned hours	65:35
● Cost per total operating cost	12%
Stores	**Typical**
● Value	$6,000,000
● SKUs	12,000
● Turnover	1.8
● Service level	91%
● Coverage	8 hr/5 day
● Staffing	4
● Stores issues/Total maintenance materials	48%

Figure 5-2. Examples of Measures to Benchmark

available. Determine whether you'll be able to glean enough from others' innovations to help your competitive position, and whether or not they'll let you look. Internal divisions and sister companies make good comparisons. It will be easy to get data, although it's unlikely you'll find many new, innovative processes.

Information from direct competitors will be difficult to come by—legally. However, industry sector leaders and businesses at large can make excellent models. They probably won't be relevant across the board, but they can inspire you to quantum leaps in selected processes. Remember the mining company that reached new heights following an airline's model of reliability.

The most important part of the benchmarking process is putting the information to use. Make it the driving force behind your plan to improve maintenance continuously. Use it to help your firm achieve a shared vision of excellence. Several companies and associations have accomplished just that. E.I. Du Pont de Nemours & Co., for one, has been benchmarking maintenance performance since 1987. There are now more than 65 Du Pont plants in North America, South America, Europe, and Japan involved. Competing companies in the petrochemical field are compared, as well as industries in other sectors. Du Pont believes that benchmarking sharpens its focus for improvement and quantifies its goals. Maintenance management in the company has been elevated to the importance it deserves. Recently, the benchmarking effort found:

- Japan and Europe use substantially more contractors than the United States.
- Japan spends less to maintain its investment, and its productivity is higher.
- Japanese companies have less stores investment with higher turnover than European and U.S. companies.

General Motors Advanced Engineering group is another example. It conducted a maintenance benchmarking study in several industries, including assembly, distribution, manufacturing, processing, and consulting/academic. The objective was to determine both the average as well as the world class measures for key parameters. Some of the more interesting findings were:

- More than half of all maintenance performed by those surveyed was reactive, whereas the world class perception was that only 18 percent should be reactive.
- Preventive maintenance averaged about one-third of the effort, with world class at just under 50 percent of all activities.
- Predictive maintenance — using machine condition data to warn of impending failure and identify defective parts — averaged only 13 percent of the total. Perceived world class was 35 percent predictive activities, representing another major gap in actual performance to a vision of the world's best.

The International Iron and Steel Institute (IISI) produced an interesting benchmark study involving 17 of its members. It concluded that maintenance in steel industries is the third highest cost item after raw materials and labor, representing between 8 percent and 15 percent of steelworks sales, and between 13 percent and 25 percent of liquid steel costs. Key recommendations to reduce these costs and improve effectiveness, based on best practices found in the study, were:

- Apply computerized maintenance management systems to control and analyze all aspects of performance.
- Ensure full and active participation of maintenance people in the design, selection, and installation of new equipment.
- Set higher maintenance standards for all work.
- Institute comprehensive condition-based monitoring and analysis.
- Employ a well-trained, multi-skilled workforce, following systematic planning and control of work.

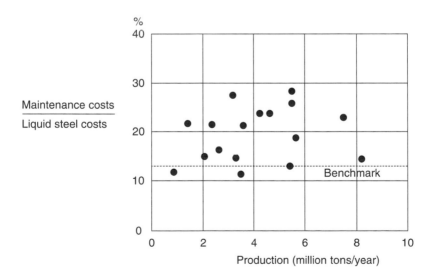

Figure 5-3. IISI Maintenance Costs Benchmark

Figure 5-3 summarizes how each of the survey participants compares against a maintenance cost benchmark. The benchmark was set as the mean minus one standard deviation.

A Coopers & Lybrand consulting study of the hydroelectric generating industry in North America came up with benchmark statistics based on thirty utilities. As with the IISI study, it averaged their results, and subtracted 1 standard deviation for the benchmark. Among the top five utilities, the average for each parameter shows:

- Maintenance costs $1,500 per megawatt installed capacity each year.
- Generation availability of 95 percent, with forced outage at 2 percent and planned outage at 3 percent.
- Emergency work at less than 3 percent, with preventive work at over 60 percent.

What all of these examples illustrate is that benchmarking produces impressive results. Apply it and you can achieve performance breakthroughs. To quote Tom Peters, "What gets measured, gets done." Let's go one step further. What gets measured and benchmarked, gets done best.

6

Management Information Systems for Maintenance

*"The amount of knowledge is not nearly as important
as the productivity of knowledge."*
Peter F. Drucker
Post-Capitalist Society

The number and complexity of equipment systems managed by a typical maintenance engineer is awesome. When you consider parts and supplies, specialist skills, and the effort required to prevent and repair problems, it is incredible that the plant usually runs. To keep it operating smoothly, you must take a systematic approach to information management.

The sheer volume of maintenance information can be staggering. An airport facility in the Far East, for example, with 7,000 equipment systems and 20,000 SKUs (stock keeping units) in maintenance stores, generates 100,000 work orders each year. At an electrical appliance manufacturing plant with 2,000 pieces of equipment and 30,000 stores SKUs, 150,000 work orders (110,000 of them "urgent") are filed annually. A public transit fleet generates 250,000 work orders or service requests for 950 vehicles. It controls 25,000 stores SKUs and has 415 tradespeople and a direct maintenance cost of $50,000,000 per year.

The number of data transactions for these businesses easily exceeds 1 million a month. With all that maintenance has to handle, they need all the help available to keep track of who is doing what tasks, on what equipment, with what parts, and at what cost. You should be using an automated information

87

management system. As discussed earlier, data about equipment histories, resource planning, scheduling for preventive and corrective maintenance, and the warranty and legal conformance routines must be documented and controlled.

Most businesses today have some sort of computerized maintenance management system (CMMS). Some have developed them in-house, but most have chosen one of the hundreds of commercially available packages. If your CMMS is more than three years old, it might benefit your company to take another look at what's available. If you don't yet have a CMMS, this chapter explains what they're all about and how to select and implement one.

OVERVIEW OF THE CMMS

In Chapter 3, we looked at various ways to enhance maintenance and materials management. Figure 6-1 shows an overview of what a typical CMMS would cover by linking the two processes. The computer program lays out the entire cycle, beginning with the requirements and ending with an analysis of purchasing and inventory control. The complete maintenance plan is addressed, from identifying what needs to be done to analyzing the completed work.

Maintenance and materials processes converge in the plant and equipment configuration and bill of materials, and in the need to report on the analysis conducted. As you can see, you can understand both systems better with this blueprint of how they interact. At the same time, the CMMS simplifies your job of managing information.

A CMMS may run on a mainframe, minicomputer, workstation, microcomputer, or network. Because of their increasing capabilities and ease in networking for multiple users, micros are now the most popular platform for the CMMS software. A typical PC-LAN (network) may have ten or fifteen users and several printers. It may be linked to other systems, particularly accounting, payroll, and inventory, if they are not part of the

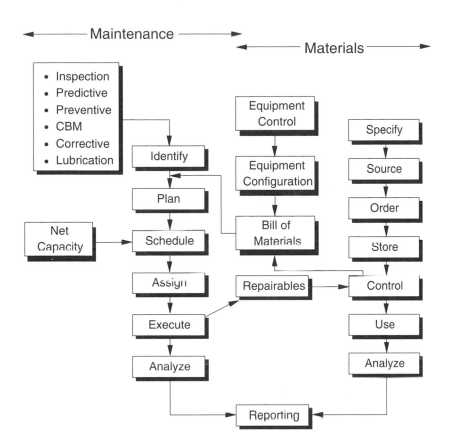

Figure 6-1. The Linked Maintenance and Materials Process

CMMS. It is usually divided into modules of related functions, which operate the various data management and analysis activities. Following is a brief description of eight of the more common modules and what they do (see Figure 6-2).

- *Equipment identification and bill of materials* — usually one of the first modules used. All the equipment covered by the CMMS is logged in with "nameplate" data. Then, the assemblies, components, and parts that make up the equipment are identified and linked according to hierarchy or relationship.

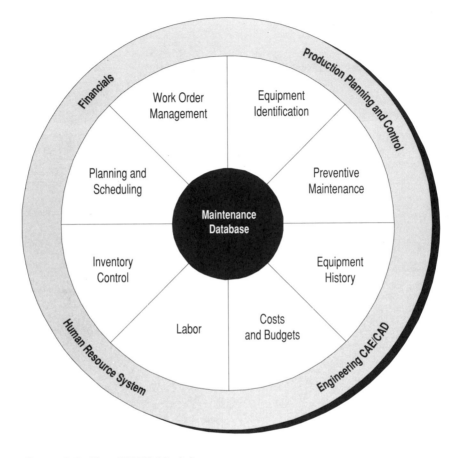

Figure 6-2. Key CMMS Modules

- *Work order management* — manages the process of opening a new order, estimating its cost, tracking its status, and ranking it according to priority.
- *Planning and scheduling* — develops task times; resources required to do the work; and schedules for all types of maintenance work, whether preventive or corrective.
- *Preventive maintenance* — a critical module that helps establish the PM schedule, describes required tasks and materials, allocates costs, and helps set schedules.

- *Inventory control* — available on most packages, it manages the stores inventory. However, many businesses use their accounting or production control software to do this job, and often on another computer. Its function is to track inventory on hand and use, costs, and allocation of inventory items used for maintenance.
- *Equipment history* — key functions are to keep histories of overhauls, repairs, costs, labor, downtime, and utilization, and to track failure causes and special events in the equipment life cycle.
- *Labor* — keeps an inventory of individuals, their skills, vacation schedules, training history, availability, and utilization to enable accurate work order and project scheduling and backlog control.
- *Costs and budgets* — most packages are able to accumulate projected and actual costs in multiple cost centers for labor, materials, services, and allocated overheads.

Depending on how sophisticated your package is, many more uses are possible, especially if it is part of a suite of other business system applications.

PROJECT MANAGING THE CMMS IMPLEMENTATION

Like other computerized systems, the CMMS must be user-driven. That is, the driving force behind it must be maintenance — the system must be useful primarily to you. The project champion should be supported by specialists in systems, materials, operations, accounting, and the like. You need a clear set of objectives that you expect from the CMMS to help guide you through the whole process. An example is shown in Figure 6-3.

Your success also hinges on knowing how to put your plan into practice. Many large businesses have developed or purchased systems delivery methodologies, which usually have a fast track for purchased packages. They are made up of a series of steps; each one must be completed before advancing to the

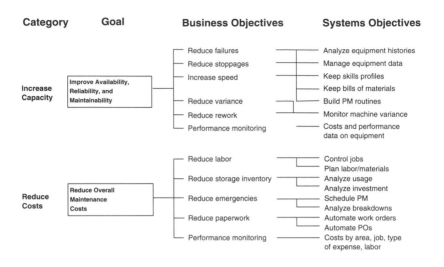

Category	Goal	Business Objectives	Systems Objectives

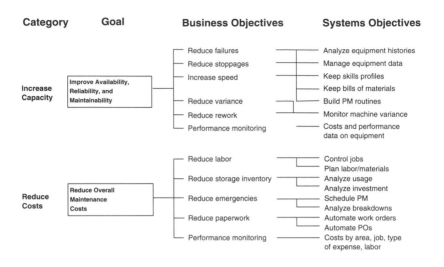

Figure 6-3. CMMS Objectives

next. An example is described in Figure 6-4, which outlines the following five phases.

- *Requirements analysis*—The first step in this phase is that your requirements be identified and documented. This should involve mapping all the processes, whether automated or manual. For example, part of the maintenance work identification process may come from condition-based monitoring. Should this information be input directly into the CMMS up front, or should you allow for manual monitoring and analysis? The result of the analysis could manually trigger a work order in the CMMS. Benchmarking and other research into the possibilities will help you decide what's best for your operation. The next step is to scout your system, both software (application) and hardware (technology), from among the many products and vendors on the market.
- *Solution definition*—This phase expands the mapping started earlier, from the required modules identified earlier to specific functions. An example of a functional

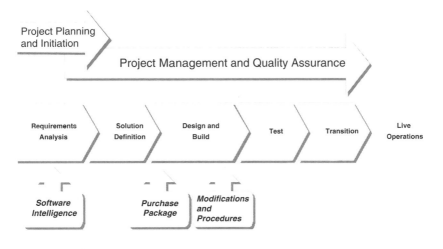

Figure 6-4. CMMS System Delivery Methodology

specification for a CMMS is presented in Appendix B. At this point, interfaces with other company systems are defined. By now, you will identify your functional requirements and which CMMS systems can meet them. Contact suppliers and ask them to submit solutions.

- *Design and build* — Next, customize and cost the package to fit your operation. When you have all your requirements designed into the solution, you can finally buy a system and have it installed and commissioned. Of course, you'll need to lay out operating procedures for data conversion, installation, and daily use. Train your staff thoroughly to reap the benefits of the system.

- *Test* — Make sure that the users, the maintenance and possibly production people, not the systems department or supplier, test the CMMS in the workplace. They are best able to judge whether it is covering the ground in maintenance management, user and technical procedures, backup and recovery, security and volume, and performance testing.

- *Transition* — This final phase is important to get your new system up and running without any major kinks. It involves converting data, installing fully the new CMMS and manual procedures, and, most importantly, handing over responsibility to the user management.

Now that you know what CMMS is and how to put it into your business, will it be worth the investment?

JUSTIFYING YOUR CMMS

A maintenance system will cost $5,000 to $250,000 for the software alone. This depends on what it can do and the hardware platform you run it on. If you consider the entire cost—customizing, interfacing with other systems, training, consulting, and communications, and the incremental hardware capacity and such add-ons as printers—it increases about five times, and this still doesn't count the cost of your own staff! A convincing case of improved maintenance productivity must be made to justify this expense.

Maintenance productivity can be defined as output divided by input. Output is measured as equipment availability, operating speed, precision, and reliability. Input is money spent on labor, materials, services, and overhead. What will the CMMS do to improve your productivity?

Failure rate and duration as well as other performance standards depend greatly on a maintenance program that is properly developed, scheduled, and executed. That, in turn, relies on equipment failure histories, records of repairs and overhauls completed, and lists of the correct materials and resources used. Minimizing downtime for inspection, repair, and overhaul requires scheduling and coordination of labor and parts.

Efficient data management clearly has an impact on maintenance output. Many companies have found that using information management produces significant results:

- Equipment effectiveness (the product of availability, speed, and precision—see Chapter 5) jumps from 50 percent to 85 percent.

- Reliability (mean time between failures) rises 20 percent.

More efficient use of labor, materials, and outside contractors often means savings of 5 percent to 15 percent of total maintenance costs. Sometimes it is difficult to attribute the savings. The CMMS acts as a new framework around which to manage maintenance. Did the savings actually come from inputting data, manipulating information, and generating reports? Or did they arise from developing and implementing a solid PM program because there was a module there that demanded to be used?

It's a moot point. Based on surveys by various software vendors, maintenance periodicals, and consultants working in the field, real benefits are achieved in both increased productivity and direct maintenance costs. One intangible benefit is often improved communication with both operations and materials, and among trades.

SOME EXAMPLES

There are about 200 CMMS packages available commercially in North America, and probably double that number when the rest of the world is included. Although most have similar broad functions, they differ greatly in user-friendliness, efficiency, platform, and operating system. Here is what six examples have to offer.

- *Chief 2000 by Maintenance Automation Corp.* — This package is in use at about 300 locations, principally in the facilities, hospital, university, and manufacturing sectors. The main platform is the PC and PC-LAN, at $12,000 for the basics, with options available. It comes with a choice of five languages (English, French, Spanish, German, and Dutch), is menu-driven, and has a custom report generator with graphics. The package has all the functions discussed earlier and includes a maintenance procedures library and several purchasing functions.

- *Maximo Series 3 by PSDI*—Maximo 3 is Windows-based, a point and click technology that is user-friendly. PSDI has about 500 locations, emphasizing manufacturing and facilities. The platform is also the PC and PC-LAN, at a cost of approximately $30,000, depending again on options. The basic package includes functions for managing fleets, as well as the procedures library. Maximo 3 is also available in five languages.

- *MPAC by the Systems Works, Inc.*—Unlike the previous two examples, the primary platform for MPAC is the minicomputer, with a significantly higher price. There are over 300 locations, focusing on utilities and process industries. They have a large research and development staff and field technical support staff. The list of available options is extensive, including tool management, warranty administration, accounting, and project planning and scheduling.

- *OOPS! by Peregrine Systems, Inc.*—This menu-driven package is one of the least expensive, at $3,500, yet rates quite high on user satisfaction surveys. Operating on a PC at 375 sites, it offers basic modules such as work orders, equipment histories, and stores inventory, but can be expanded with options. Users are mainly in manufacturing and facilities.

- *COMPASS by Bonner & Moore, Inc.*—The COMPASS system operates on an IBM-compatible mainframe, and it is expensive—about $100,000 for the basic software. It has numerous functions and is available in four languages. Of the 150 or so operating sites, most are in the process industries.

- *MMS by MARCAM Corporation*—Installed in over 400 sites, mostly in manufacturing, facilities, and processing, this software operates in a client-server environment on Windows. It is available in English, Spanish, German, and French. What is provided is quite extensive, and is comprehensive for materials management functions.

Whichever package solution you eventually purchase, it is a good idea to buy the maintenance contract as well. First, it ensures that your software will remain current with the periodic updates issued. Second, if you become an active participant in the software company's user conferences, you can influence the direction these updates take. The maintenance option is usually about 10 percent to 15 percent of the software cost. Another point worth considering: If your industry is strongly represented in the customer listing, updates will likely be geared to your special needs.

An interesting case study for CMMS application is Molson's Brewery in Canada. Now the largest in that country, it has plants in every region, coast to coast. The brewing industry in Canada consists of many medium and small plants in each province because, according to provincial law, beer must be made where it is sold.

In the early 1980s, each of Molson's plants had their own local maintenance approach. They had time-based preventive maintenance programs, corrective maintenance for breakdowns, and overhauls during scheduled shutdowns. Systems were ad hoc, both manual and automated. In the mid 1980s, the engineering group recognized the potential cost savings and capacity improvement by making three changes in the way in which maintenance was managed. First, fix the process; second, automate it; and third, get leverage by doing it the same way in all the plants.

They developed a systematic approach to work order management, PM development, and maintenance stores management. They purchased IBM S36 minicomputers and the ShawWare (MARCAM) maintenance and materials management package. After a blitz of implementation, improvements were achieved in the planning and control of maintenance. With the usual promotions and engineering staff turnover, the implementation slowed without the full integration of the process and systems being accomplished. Further, Molson's underwent a merger with Carling O'Keefe, the third largest brewery in

Canada. The restructuring was comprehensive, with complete integration of operations.

In the early 1990s, it was difficult to get vendor support of the S36s and their application programs, and there was a need for upgrading. IBM AS400s replaced the less capable S36s, and the manufacturing, financial, and CMMS systems were upgraded as well. A network, shown in Figure 6-5, was established, linking the largest of the eight regional plants. The CMMS configuration in these plants is now:

- 5 AS400 minis.
- 120 PC/terminals.
- 30 laser printers.
- Networked across all functions and all locations.

The capital cost for the project totaled over $3.5 million. This included software, hardware, networking, consulting, and in-house information technology staff. In addition, three user

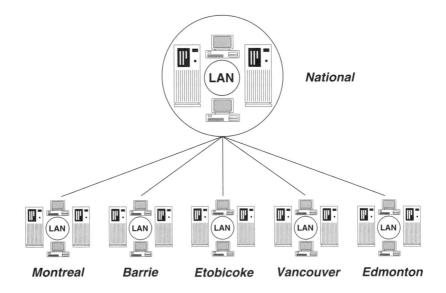

Figure 6-5. Molson Information Technology Network

representatives were assigned full time—a champion from maintenance engineering, a storage inventory specialist, and a systems application specialist. With this investment, Molson's senior management was looking for quantifiable returns. After the first two years (1993–1994) of implementation, improvements in plant performance and cost reductions have been excellent, near the $3.5 million capital cost.

- Equipment effectiveness is up.
- Overtime is down.
- Maintenance productivity is up at the three largest plants.
- Stores inventory savings were substantial.
- Other savings are being realized in purchasing efficiency, reduced overhauls, and staff effectiveness.

The project champion is confident that these savings will grow as the remaining plants take full advantage of the system capabilities. Maintenance costs currently represent about 16 percent of operating costs across their plants, and their vision is to reduce this to 12 percent over the next three years—the number achieved by their best plant. He believes that the main reasons for this success were supportive management, accountability for results, and a true vendor partnership with the software company.

Molson's hasn't stopped here. They are currently working on an executive information system to make the CMMS even more effective for the area managers. Other initiatives include direct integration of condition monitoring and capital project management.

With the rapid expansion of microtechnology, functions and features only dreamed about a few years ago are now common. Scanning of documents into memory; pen data entry; expert diagnostic systems; total bar code entry; and remote, portable wireless terminals are used in many sectors. To keep pace with all that technology has to offer at the best price, periodically review the latest CMMS packages.

Part III

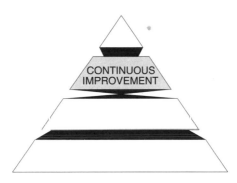

CONTINUOUS
IMPROVEMENT

7

Reliability Centered Maintenance

"The more unstable the system, the more chance matters."
Alvin Toffler
Power Shift

To be competitive, industry must continually improve. Companies are embracing, like never before, efficiency methods such as just-in-time and total quality management. These structured, step-by-step systems can both identify and help implement ways to enhance the business. They are tools to build on and make better use of employees' operating abilities and technology know-how.

Maintenance, too, is being changed by the competitive pressures in the marketplace. It also has much to learn from the new techniques that are transforming business practice. And those who use them properly are finding that better maintenance can mean bigger profits.

There are several techniques that apply to maintenance performance. Their common goal is to continually improve that performance by:

- Dealing with each type of failure most appropriately, in the most cost-effective way.
- Enhancing productivity with a more proactive and planned approach.
- Ensuring active support and cooperation of people from maintenance, materials, operations, technical, and administrative functions.

103

One of the most notable techniques is reliability centered maintenance (RCM). By providing a strategic framework and using the knowledge and expertise of people in the organization, it can accomplish two important goals. First, it identifies the maintenance requirements of a physical asset that meet the operational or production goals. Then it optimizes the performance, with real results.

RCM works in a progression of related steps. First, it examines the functions and associated productivity goals of the asset. Second, it assesses the ways those goals can fall short and the effects of failing. Finally, RCM's detective work deduces the most feasible and effective ways to eliminate or reduce the consequences of failure.

RCM was launched in the U.S. commercial airline industry during the early 1960s. It developed in response to rapidly increasing maintenance costs, poor availability, and concern over the effectiveness of traditional time-based preventive maintenance. The problems were obvious, so was the need — more reliable maintenance programs.

Studies were conducted of existing engineering techniques and preventive maintenance practices, which we discussed earlier in Chapter 4 under maintenance tactics. The results revealed two surprising facts about the traditional, time-based, preventive maintenance approach:

1. Scheduled overhaul has little effect on the overall reliability of a complex item, unless failure is frequent.
2. There are many items for which there is no effective form of scheduled maintenance.

The results of these initial studies have extended far beyond the airlines. They were used to develop the basis of a logical preventive maintenance program that can apply throughout industry. This approach has since become known as reliability centered maintenance.

RCM was first applied on a large scale to develop the maintenance program of the Boeing 747. Later, it was used for the L-1011 and DC-10. The results have been impressive. These aircraft achieved significant reductions in scheduled or time-based maintenance, with no decrease in reliability. For example, only 66,000 labor hours of structural inspections were required before first heavy inspection at 20,000 flying hours on the Boeing 747, as compared to 4,000,000 labor hours over same period on the smaller DC-8. On the DC-10, only seven items were subject to scheduled overhaul, in comparison with the scheduled overhaul of 339 items on the DC-8.

RCM (or MSG-3 as it is known in the aerospace industry) is now used to develop the maintenance programs for all major types of aircraft. Other applications include the navy, utilities, the offshore oil industry, and manufacturing processes. RCM is particularly suitable where large, complex equipment is used and where equipment failures pose significant economic, safety, or environmental risks.

CREATING VALUE FOR CUSTOMERS

As desirable as it may be to have a comprehensive, logically based maintenance program, it is of little use unless it helps maintenance, and the company as a whole, create value for its customers and shareholders. Typical benefits of RCM are outlined in Figure 7-1. The advantages of instituting an RCM program depend on the nature of the business, the risks posed by equipment failures, and the state of the existing maintenance program.

RCM ELEMENTS: PHILOSOPHY TO PRACTICE

RCM is based on the philosophy that maintenance is a key function of the company. It is crucial for the expected functional performance and productivity goals to be achieved. Further, maintenance requirements are best developed by multidisciplinary teams from production, materials, maintenance, and technical departments, and should be founded on a logical, structural, and engineered approach. Some of the key precepts

Quality	Service	Cost	Time	Risk
Increased Plant Availability (2-10%) Elimination of chronic failures and inherent reliability problems Flexibility to accommodate production requirements Documented bases for maintenance program Improved ownership for maintenance program	Better teamwork and communication Improved understanding of "customer" requirements Less disruption of production processes due to unplanned breakdowns	Optimized maintenance program Reduced levels of scheduled maintenance (10-50%) Better maintenance contract administration. Clear guidelines for application of new maintenance technology. Longer life of expensive equipment. Reduction in secondary damage	Shorter repair times Reduced duration of scheduled overhauls Extended periods between overhauls (60-300%)	Safety & environmental integrity a priority Failures with unacceptable consequences must be dealt with Reduced likelihood of multiple failures Reduced numbers of routine, invasive tasks Reduced risk to plant maintenance workers

Figure 7-1. Benefits of Reliability Centered Maintenance

of RCM are that equipment redundancy should be eliminated, where appropriate; condition-based or predictive maintenance tactics are favored over traditional time-based methods; and run-to-failure is acceptable, where warranted.

To develop an RCM-based maintenance program for physical resources, we need to answer the following questions:

1. What assets are owned and operated by the company and to which of these should RCM be applied?
2. What are the functions and performance expectations of a selected asset?

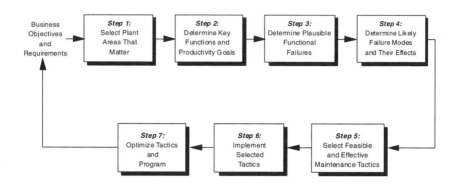

Figure 7-2. RCM Review Process

3. In what ways can it fail to perform these functions?
4. What causes it to fail?
5. What are the consequences of each failure?
6. What should be done to prevent each failure, and what steps should be taken if effective preventive measures can't be found?

These questions are answered through a logical, seven-step review process, illustrated in Figure 7-2. The process begins with an understanding of the business requirements and objectives. This ensures that the maintenance program meets the productivity goals for the physical resource under review.

The maintenance agenda is then defined. Once that happens, an ongoing monitoring and review process is established to make the most of the program. The major steps in the RCM review process are described below.

Step 1: Select Plant Areas That Matter

Businesses typically have thousands of pieces of machinery and equipment. These can range from pumps and valves to process systems, rolling mills, fleets of load-haul-dump (LHD) trucks, ships, or buildings. They may be fixed or mobile. Each asset will benefit from RCM in varying degrees.

Therefore, the first step in the RCM process is to identify and prioritize the physical resources owned or operated by the enterprise. Only then can they be reviewed properly. This initial stage involves:

- Establishing a structured, comprehensive list of all physical assets owned or used by the organization that require some form of maintenance or engineering attention. This list is referred to as the plant register, plant inventory, or equipment family tree.
- Assessing the impact of the physical resources on the key business performance areas. These may include availability, process capability, quality, cost, and safety or environmental risk. This ensures that the review focuses on the areas or equipment in the plant that could benefit most from RCM. Although several complementary methods can be used in the assessment, the precise method is not critical. Of more importance is selecting a method, documenting it and its results, and then proceeding with the review. Simplicity is the key. Usually, the highest and lowest priority systems will be obvious. It's not worth the added effort to figure out the exact order of importance of those between the two.
- Establishing the boundaries between equipment systems. Boundaries include everything necessary for the physical resource to do its job. This helps define the scope of the review and organizes it into manageable pieces.

One company selected its environmental control and monitoring equipment, including dust collectors and effluent samplers. They concluded that this category represented the greatest long-term risk.

Step 2: Determine Key Functions and Productivity Goals

Once the physical resource is selected, its functions and associated productivity goals are determined. This is a key step.

The purpose of a maintenance tactic is to make sure the equipment is working properly and producing on schedule.

Every physical asset has a function—usually several. These can be categorized as:

- *Primary*—This is why the equipment exists at all. It is usually evident from its name, as well as from the interfaces that are supported between physical assets. An example of a conveyer's primary function, for instance, is to transfer rock from hopper to crusher at a minimum rate of 10 tons/hour.
- *Secondary*—In addition to its primary purpose, a physical asset usually has a number of secondary functions. These are sometimes less obvious, but the consequences of failure may be no less severe. Examples of secondary functions include maintaining a pressure boundary, relaying local or control room indications, supplying structural support, or providing isolation.
- *Protective*—As processes and equipment increase in complexity, so do the ways in which they can fail dramatically. Likewise, the consequences of failure. To mitigate these dire results, protective devices are used. The job of these devices must be defined before adequate maintenance programs can be developed. Typical protective functions include warning operators of abnormal conditions, automatically shutting down a piece of equipment, and taking over a function that has failed.

In addition to defining the functions, this process highlights the expected level of performance or the productivity goals. These can include capacity, reliability, availability, product quality, and safety and environmental standards.

While this may sound relatively straightforward, technical and maintenance performance are typically judged differently. Thus, performance can be defined as:

- *Built-in or inherent*—what it can do.

- *Required* — what we want it to do.
- *Actual* — what it is doing.

In many instances, the equipment can deliver what is required of it with proper maintenance. Situations can arise, though, where what's required exceeds what the physical resource is capable of. In these cases, maintenance cannot meet the performance levels.

If there is a big gap between the performance needed and the built-in ability or the performance currently being achieved, the equipment asset needs to be modified. Either it should be replaced with a more capable item, or operating changes must be made to reduce expectations.

Again, the purpose of the RCM review is to define the maintenance requirements for a physical asset that are necessary to meet the business objectives. The level of performance, then, reflects what is required or wanted from the asset.

Step 3: Determine Plausible Functional Failures

The third step is to address all plausible ways in which equipment can perform below expectations. Partial and total shortcomings are considered, as well as an inadvertent function.

Usually, we tend to think of an item failing when it stops working — a go/no-go situation. For example, the car doesn't start or a compressor doesn't provide high pressure air. While some equipment is like this, notably electronic machinery, in other cases what constitutes a failure is less clear. Your car may start and run, but its acceleration is poor and it uses too much gas. The compressor may run but does it provide enough air pressure or volume?

Obviously, an idea of the boundary between acceptable and unacceptable performance is needed to determine when failure occurs. This boundary is the expected level of performance. The definition of functional failure is the inability of a physical asset to deliver its expected level of performance.

This definition suggests that a function could fail in numerous ways, each with its own (usually different) modes and effects. This happens because there may be:

- A total loss of function, where the item stops working altogether. For example, a pumping system fails to provide any flow.
- A partial loss of function, where the item works but fails to achieve the expected level of performance. For example, a pumping system fails to provide an adequate flow.
- Multiple levels of performance expected from an individual function.

The expected level of performance defines not only what is considered a failure, but the amount of maintenance needed to avoid that failure. As illustrated in Figure 7-3, this frequently creates conflict between various departments. It is essential, then, that all concerned — the technical, operations, and maintenance departments — play a part in drafting the performance levels. A joint seal of approval is essential before proceeding.

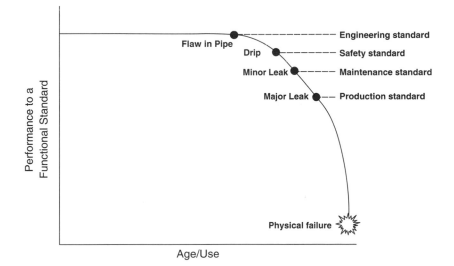

Figure 7-3. Performance Standards and Function Failure

Step 4: Determine Likely Failure Modes and Their Effects

The next task is to set forth the likely failure modes and their cause and effect. A failure mode describes what can or has happened as opposed to what caused it to happen. For example, one failure mode of a pump could be a seized bearing that halts any flow.

Failure modes are spelled out because the process of anticipating, preventing, detecting, and correcting failures is applied to any number of different examples. While many potential failure modes can be listed, only those that are fairly likely need be considered. These include:

- Failure modes that have occurred on the same or similar equipment. This is determined through a review of maintenance work order history and experience.
- Failure modes that are already the subject of preventive maintenance tasks.
- Other failure modes that have not happened but are considered possible because of experience or vendor/manufacturer recommendations. The extent to which these less-than-likely failure modes are included will depend on their consequences. The greater the potential setback, the more these "what if" scenarios count.

Possible causes of the particular failure are also identified since they have a direct bearing on the maintenance tactics used. In the example of the seized bearing, the cause of this failure could be a lack of lubrication. Other typical reasons are wear, erosion, corrosion, fatigue, dirt, incorrect operation, or faulty assembly.

What actually happens when each failure mode occurs is next identified. The effects are described fully, as if nothing were done to prevent the failure. This way, the consequences can be judged fairly. To do so, the following are described:

- The evidence of failure to the operating crew under normal conditions.

- The hazards the failure may pose to worker safety, public safety, process stability, or the environment.
- The effect on production output and maintenance.

Step 5: Select Feasible and Effective Maintenance Tactics

Failures of the physical resources owned or used by a company can vary enormously. Their results may be potentially catastrophic — or trivial. How great the impact influences the way the company views the failure and the steps deemed necessary to prevent it, such as adding backup systems. In some cases, it may not be worth the effort and expense. To successfully manage a failure, the preventive maintenance tactic must be:

- *Technically feasible* — dealing effectively with the technical characteristics of the failure.
- *Cost-effective* — reducing or avoiding pitfalls in line with dollar and operating constraints.

Tactical options are discussed more fully in Chapter 4.

Whether a particular approach is technically appropriate to solve the failure depends not only on the kind of help, but the nature of the problem. Technically feasible tactics for condition-based and time-based maintenance satisfy the following criteria.

1. *Condition-based*
    — It is possible to detect a physical resource's degraded condition or performance.
    — The failure is predictable as it progresses from first instance to complete breakdown.
    — It is practical to monitor the physical resource in less time than it takes for the problem to develop completely.
    — The time between incipient and functional failure is long enough to be of some use — that is, actions can be taken to avoid the failure.

2. *Time-based*
   — There is an identifiable point at which the physical asset shows a rapid increase in failure rate.
   — Most assets survive to that age. For failures with significant safety or environmental risks, there should be no failures before this point.
   — The task restores the asset's condition. (This might mean partial restoration if the asset is overhauled, for example, or complete restoration if the item is discarded and replaced.)

To be cost-effective, preventive maintenance must reduce the likelihood and/or consequences of failure to acceptable levels, be readily implemented, and stay within budget. Within these limits, a maintenance tactic is considered cost-effective if:

- For hidden problems, it cuts the chance of a multiple failure to an acceptable level.
- For failures with safety and environmental effects, the risks are kept to a comfortable minimum.
- For failures with production setbacks, the cost of the tactic is, over time, less than the production losses. Also, it must be cheaper than repairing the problem it is meant to prevent.
- For failures with maintenance consequences, the cost of prevention measures is, over time, less than repairing the failure that would otherwise result.

If maintenance measures are neither technically feasible nor cost-effective, then, depending on the risk of failure, one of the following default actions is selected:

- For hidden failures, a failure-finding tactic to reduce the likelihood of multiple failures. An example is testing the readiness of standby equipment.
- For failures with unacceptable safety or environmental risks, redesign or modification.
- For failures with production or maintenance consequences, run-to-failure or corrective maintenance.

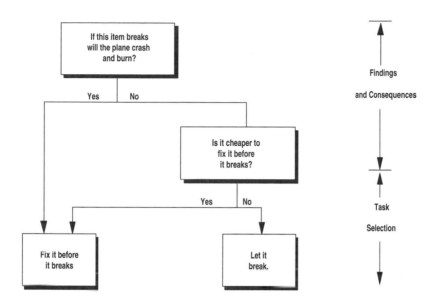

Figure 7-4. Simplified Maintenance Selection Logic Diagram

A logic tree diagram is used to integrate the consequences of failure with technically feasible and cost-effective maintenance tactics. A simplified version of this diagram is illustrated in Figure 7-4. In general, tactics to prevent failures follow this order:

- *Condition-based maintenance (CBM) tactics* — These generally have the least impact on production, help focus corrective actions, and get the most out of the economic life of the equipment.
- *Time-based repair/restoration tactics* — These may work for failures that present a significant safety, environmental, or economic risk to the organization. However, this approach is less preferable than CBM for a number of reasons. It usually affects production or operations, the age-limit can mean premature removals, and the additional shop work required increases the cost of maintenance.
- *Time-based discard tactics* — These are generally the least cost-effective preventive maintenance measures. They

tend to be used, though, where repair or restoration is impossible or ineffective, such as for components like filter elements, o-rings, and, in some cases, integrated circuit boards.

- *Combinations* — In some cases a combination of tactics may be necessary to reduce the safety and environmental risks to an acceptable level. In general, this involves a condition-based maintenance method along with some form of time-based maintenance. An example would be the in-place inspection of an aircraft engine by borescope every 50 flying hours, combined with time-based inspection and overhaul in a shop every 200 hours.

Once the maintenance tactics have been chosen, next comes deciding how often they are performed initially. For condition-based tactics, the frequency is linked to the technical characteristics of the failure and the specific monitoring technique. Depending on these factors, the time can vary from weeks to months. Generally, the more sophisticated (and expensive) the technique, the more infrequent.

Time-based tactics are applied according to the expected useful life of the physical asset. That is determined by the age at which wear-out begins, when the chance of failure greatly increases. How often the failure-finding tactic is needed depends on how available it is and how likely a breakdown in the system.

Figure 7-5 gives an example of how the first five steps might look on a worksheet.

Step 6: Implement Selected Tactics

It often requires as much effort — and more coordination — to put the results of the RCM in motion than the review itself. The recommendations are compared with the tasks already included in the maintenance program. The question is whether to add new tasks, change the existing ones (scope or frequency), and/or delete any.

Equipment: Family Car Assembly: Braking Component: Front Disc Brakes							
Function	**Failure**	**Cause**	**Effect**	**Criticality**			
				Severity	Frequency	Ease of finding	Overall Factor
1. To stop car smoothly within 20m from speed of 60km/hr on dry pavement on brake pedal application of 3cm. 2. - - - 3. - - - 4. - - -	1.1 - - - 1.2 - - - 1.3 - - - 1.4 Brake pedal moves to more than 3cm to stop	1.4.1 - - - 1.4.2 - - - 1.4.3 Hydraulic fluid level low, caused by leakage in system, which causes pedal to move 5 to 8cm before braking action.	1.4.3 Stopping becomes increasingly difficult with more pressure application of brake pedal required; fluid continues to leak until pedal pressure has no effect on calipers to close disc pads. Car fails to stop, resulting in severe safety hazard.	High (5)	Low (1)	Medium (3)	Moderate (15)

Maintenance Task	**Schedule**	**Responsibility**	**Comments**
1.4.3 ● Monitor brake pedal movement ● Monitor brake fluid level and top up ● Check braking hydraulic system for signs of wear, corrosion, leaks	● Measure quarterly ● 15,000 km intervals ● 30,000 km intervals	● Operator ● Operator ● Mechanic	● Family car has few operators. Small changes likely to be detected ● If topped off twice in one year, refer to mechanic. ● Check pads and rotor at the same time.

Figure 7-5. RCM Worksheet

Next on the agenda are the actions needed to put the maintenance tactics into effect. These may include:

- Tweaking maintenance schedules.
- Developing or revising task instructions.
- Specifying spare parts and adjusting inventory levels.
- Acquiring diagnostic or test equipment.
- Revising operation and maintenance procedures.
- Specifying the need for repair or restoration procedures.
- Most significantly, conducting training in the new procedures.

To ensure all this is coordinated smoothly, an integrated plan is developed. This plan underscores the actions required and assigns responsibilities and target dates for their completion.

Step 7: Optimize Tactics and Program

Once the RCM review is complete and the maintenance work identified, periodic adjustments are made. The process is responsive to changes in plant design, operating conditions, maintenance history, and discovered conditions. In particular, the frequency of the tactics is adjusted to reflect the operating and maintenance history of the physical resource. The objectives of this ongoing activity are to reduce equipment failure, improve preventive maintenance effectiveness and the use of resources, identify the need to expand the review, and react to changing industry or economic conditions.

To achieve these goals, two complementary activities are integrated into a "living program."

1. The periodic re-assessment and revision of the RCM review results. The frequency of re-assessment depends to some degree on the equipment age but is usually conducted every two to five years.
2. A continuous process of monitoring, feedback, and adaptation. This process analyzes and assesses the data produced by production and maintenance activities for failure rates, causes, and trends. It includes variances between actual and target performance. Corrective actions can then be taken. These may include changing the task type, scope, or frequency; revising procedures; providing additional training; or changing the design.

Continually reviewing and improving the initial maintenance program is akin to a quality management process that continuously improves product quality.

IMPLEMENTING RCM

Some of the key success factors in previous RCM programs are listed in Figure 7-6. To achieve such success and manage change effectively, the RCM program must be phased in and constantly improved.

The continuous improvement strategy is long-term, involving people from production, materials, maintenance, and technical functions in the RCM review process. The program

- Clear project goals
- Management support and a commitment to introduce a controlled maintenance environment
- Union involvement
- Good understanding of RCM philosophy by plant staff
- Pilot RCM applications to demonstrate success and build support
- Sufficient resources for both the review and subsequent implementation of recommendations
- Clear documentation of results to facilitate acceptance of recommendations
- Integration with condition-based maintenance capability

Figure 7-6. RCM Program Key Success Factors

involves the use of a part-time review team, under the direction of a full-time facilitator. As a result, it can take a few years to review the critical physical resources in a company.

This approach complements other improvement initiatives, such as just in time (JIT) and total quality management (TQM). It provides:

- A high degree of support from people in production, materials, maintenance, and technical departments for RCM, ensuring acceptance of change.
- Many part-time review teams under the direction of a full-time facilitator to review important plant areas. Thus, it is easier to obtain the right people to conduct the review.
- Flexibility and cost-effectiveness, minimizing the need for full-time staff.

The basic building block of this strategy is the cross-functional RCM review team of company employees. The RCM review process addresses six questions about a physical asset (see p. 106). To answer these questions, input is required not only from maintenance but also the production, materials, and technical departments. As a result, the RCM review is best conducted by small teams (five to seven members), with at least one member from each of the above functions who is knowledgeable about the physical resource under consideration. The other key member of the review team is the facilitator who provides expertise in the RCM methodology and guides the review process.

The RCM review teams meet on a part-time basis. Typically, this involves one to two meetings per week of about three hours duration each. Team members also spend about three to four hours per meeting on individual preparatory or follow-up work. The RCM review process takes about 10 to 15 meetings to complete. The physical resource chosen may be studied in sections, by subgroups, so that the review can be accomplished in this time.

The RCM review team also coordinates how the recommendations are carried out. Team meetings during this phase are of similar duration but less frequent. In addition, a phased-in approach is used to manage change successfully. This approach is employed to:

- Establish the need for RCM and build support for its implementation.
- Establish a vision of excellence.
- Customize RCM methods to meld with existing structures and systems.
- Promote technology transfer and commitment to RCM through an initial cadre of people trained and experienced in its methods.
- Achieve immediate results to build credibility.

The major phases in this implementation approach and general tasks are illustrated in Figure 7-7.

The following is an example of the use of RCM in manufacturing. One mining company with a fleet of 240 ton trucks in continuous operation wanted to reduce unplanned downtime. They analyzed the data in the truck dispatch system to determine the highest delay causes, and selected an assembly

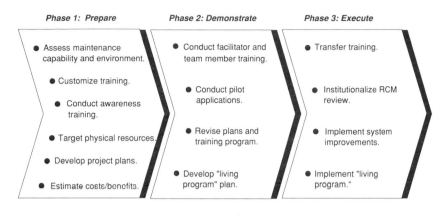

Figure 7-7. RCM Implementation Phases

that was both significant and reasonably straightforward. Their choice was the hydraulic box dump assembly.

With a team of in-pit and shop maintainers led by a facilitator with RCM expertise, they met for about two to three hours every week over thirteen weeks. The primary function was defined as: "Provide hydraulic power to smoothly and symmetrically raise and lower a loaded (240t) dump tray. The maximum overall cycle is 47 seconds for an empty tray at the regulated pressure of 2400 psi ± 50 psi with the prime mover at 1910 rpm." This function is stated crisply, with several standards of performance that make the definition of a function failure clear:

- Fails to raise the dump tray at all with a regulated pressure of 2400 ± 50 psi.
- Tray is raised too slowly (overall cycle time > 47s empty) at a pressure of less than 2350 psi.
- Tray is raised too slowly (overall cycle time > 47s empty) at a pressure of less than 2400 psi but with the engine less than 1910 rpm.
- Tray is raised erratically.
- Tray cannot be raised to full height.
- Tray is lowered too slowly.

About 150 modes of failure were determined using cause-effect diagrams and then transcribed to worksheets using terse phrases such as "Hoist control valve spool jammed by foreign material or wear and tear."

The failure effects were classed as to degree of severity using a frequency and severity matrix, with a bias toward frequency, on the assumption that if you take care of the chronic problems, the acute ones will take care of themselves. The effect corresponding to the jammed spool above is "Sufficient pilot pressure not available to move dump control valve spool and so tray cannot be lifted. The pilot valve is changed, which requires two labor hours and the truck is down for less than four hours."

The cost-effectiveness of this RCM example is clear. Downtime costs about 500 tons/hour and is worth $20,000 in lost production, or $480,000 in a one-day period. They were able to find the root causes of all critical failures, change both maintenance and operating procedures to reduce the incidence of some causes, and make some simple modifications in hydraulic system design to eliminate others.

Today's challenging maintenance environment demands continuous improvement. RCM provides a strategic framework to do just that. If properly applied, its benefits can be seen in better service and products. RCM is a logical and structural approach to balancing resources with the equipment reliability requirements.

Although it clearly involves the help of several functions in the organization, it is very much "top-down" and engineering oriented. The next chapter describes a maintenance philosophy that is "bottom-up" and has as its foundation employee involvement.

8
Total Productive Maintenance

"How much should one maintain one's own motorcycle? It seems natural and normal to me to make use of the small tool kits and instruction booklets supplied with each machine, and keep it tuned and adjusted myself ... there is no manual that deals with the real business of motorcycle maintenance, the most important aspect of all. Caring about what you are doing is considered either unimportant or taken for granted."

Robert M. Pirsig
Zen and the Art of Motorcycle Maintenance

No matter what a physical resource can do, it will be only as effective as the person who operates it. Total product maintenance (TPM) is an approach to managing physical assets that emphasizes the importance of operator involvement in making equipment reliable. *Caring* about the job cannot be taught. But TPM creates an environment that encourages that kind of commitment.

Management has always held an operator accountable for production output. More than ever, that person is also responsible now for product quality. Many factors affect how well that can be achieved, including the way in which the workplace is organized as well as the equipment's effectiveness. When several people are involved, producing quality depends on teamwork.

TPM makes it more realistic for individual operators and the group to meet their primary goal — to produce quality products, at the time and the rate required. In its broadest sense, TPM is based on three sets of principles.

1. *Maintenance engineering* — Equipment and machinery for all purposes is becoming increasingly complex, with designed-in obsolescence. Maintenance engineering, once a subunit of general engineering, seeks to manage the equipment life cycle, from strategic asset planning,

through design and construction, to operations, maintenance and disposal. Several techniques characterize the proactive nature of maintenance engineering, including:
- Preventive (or planned) maintenance:
    Planned and scheduled maintenance activities to find and correct problems that could lead to failure
- Predictive and condition-based maintenance:
    Reducing fixed-time maintenance and relying on the condition of the equipment to determine maintenance activity
- Productive (or proactive) maintenance and cost reduction:
    Maximizing equipment performance through reliability and maintainability improvement and failure analysis
- Equipment data management:
    Equipment configuration, bills of material, "as is" engineering drawings and maintenance histories
- Life cycle costing:
    The complete cost of equipment, from design and specification through construction and procurement to operations, maintenance, and disposal

2. *Total quality management (TQM)* — Total quality concepts were developed after World War II and wholeheartedly adopted by Japanese manufacturing to improve the global image and acceptance of their products. Based on the shop floor, where all employees contributed to small, incremental improvements in product quality at each stage of the process, it grew to encompass every aspect of the business. Therefore, small groups of employees in production, marketing, accounting, information systems, personnel, and every other department used problem identification and problem solving tools and techniques to provide a higher quality service or product to their "customer." The ultimate goal of TQM is zero defects. Management style in a TQM culture is participative, trusting, and focused on fixing problems

and defects, not on apportioning blame. Information is widely shared, and TQM people let the data lead them.

3. *Just-in-time (JIT)*—Just-in-time has as its goal the elimination of all waste: wasted time, space, labor, materials, inventory, movement. Anything that does not add value in the eyes of the customer adds waste. So transforming metal into implements adds value. Moving the work-in-process from one workstation to an inventory pile, then from that pile to another workstation doesn't add value; therefore, it adds waste. The core concept for JIT is the reduction of the cycle time. Focusing on time to process and reducing this time has the effect of reducing inventory, delays, labor and space. Procedures are optimized, standardized, and taught. Lot sizes are reduced. Flexibility is dramatically increased.

TPM, as it is practiced now, began in Japan as a vital and necessary response to business imperatives to reduce waste, product variation, and production cycle times. It was a fresh approach to the new challenges of the marketplace, not a logical progression of systematic maintenance management.

Traditionally, maintenance was expected to keep a plant or an individual machine available for a targeted period of scheduled time, say, 90 percent. Because of work-in-process inventories, most machines could be considered independent. If several machines in a series were maintained at 90 percent, the availability of the series was 90 percent because of this independence. If a machine varied much from the norm, the problem would eventually be noticed in final product quality inspection and traced back to the offending machine. Maintenance would then make the correction.

Just-in-time techniques, though, attacked all forms of waste—anything that did not add value to the manufacturing process. This meant the end of idle work-in-process inventories. The machines in a sequential process became interdependent.

Under these circumstances, the success of the entire process relied on each machine working to a uniform plant load, or drumbeat. Thus, a six-machine process, with each machine maintained at 90 percent, no longer meant 90 percent availability overall, but 90 percent times itself 6 times — $(90\%)^6$ or 53 percent!

To further complicate matters for maintenance, final quality control inspection was being moved upstream in the process, to eliminate defects and yield fluctuations at their source. As a result, machine performance problems were being identified much earlier. Demands for conformance and reliability were greatly increased, with more stringent variation checks.

Maintenance management — or, more correctly, the management of equipment effectiveness — had to adapt quickly to the new directives. The concept that evolved was TPM, sometimes known by its most prominent feature, autonomous (operator) maintenance.

OBJECTIVES AND THEMES OF TPM

The prime objectives of total productive maintenance are to:

- Maximize equipment effectiveness and productivity, and eliminate all machine losses.
- Create a sense of ownership in equipment operators through a program of training and involvement.
- Promote continuous improvement through small-group activities involving production, engineering, and maintenance personnel.

Each enterprise has its own unique definition and vision for TPM, but in most cases there are common elements and themes. There are seven broad elements in any TPM program. These have been summarized in the TPM wheel in Figure 8-1.

Asset Strategy

TPM is commonly used to support and enable the principles of JIT and TQM. This usually involves moving some

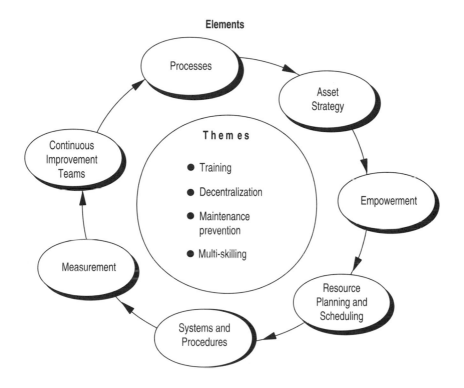

Figure 8-1. The TPM Wheel

equipment into a cell arrangement and removing anything that is redundant. Setup modifications and upgrading machine requirements are also commonly part of the plan.

Simplifying, streamlining, and automating the manufacturing process have an impact on the way maintenance is conducted. It is crucial, therefore, to dovetail the maintenance strategy — described in Chapter 1 — with the new asset structure.

When JIT is introduced, maintenance management normally should be involved immediately in:

- *Layout evaluations* — including maintainability, operability, hydraulic/pneumatic/electrical/steam/plumbing services, environmental concerns, and floor loading considerations.
- *Equipment modifications* — such as solving chronic problems before a cell startup. This could also mean providing enablers, for example, color-coded service lines and machine air lifts, and reducing excess motion to reduce wear and noise.
- *Post-move services* — to restore the equipment to satisfactory operating condition as a cell is formed. Of key importance is the initiation or revision of a specific *preventive maintenance program*.

Empowerment

TPM puts the power to improve in the employees' hands. It grants workers autonomy, along with responsibility. At the same time, TPM recognizes that employees in one area have much to teach and learn from others. The entire organization gains strength and ideas from motivated continuous improvement teams.

A TPM environment encourages a skills exchange between operators and maintenance, and multi-skill training in the various crafts. It can provide increased job satisfaction for operations, trades, engineers, and supervision alike. But the organization arrangements must be planned carefully. Change management and multi-skilling were discussed in Chapter 2.

What is really exciting about TPM is that it can fundamentally change organization culture. Centralized, *command and control* maintenance structures cannot support a JIT/TQM/TPM initiative.

Operator ownership is not about boundaries or barriers around equipment or sections of the process. It's an expression of commitment and caring about conditions, causes, and effects. Building operator ownership is mostly a matter of removing impediments and providing correct training and tools to encourage a supportive relationship that is technically informed.

Resource Planning and Scheduling

During the introduction of TPM, there will be significantly increased demand on the maintenance department, especially as operators train to be more equipment conscious. As they discover the causes of chronic equipment losses or malfunctions, they will want to have them corrected quickly.

If these operators are to be enthusiastic partners in equipment care, the maintenance department must have planning and scheduling procedures in place. They must have the capacity and skills available to assign priorities and carry out the work quickly and professionally. As many organizations have found, it helps to dedicate specific tradespersons to particular areas. In this way, they become familiar with the equipment and form closer ties with the operators and supervisors.

Systems and Procedures

As continuous improvement teams begin to focus on equipment performance, standard *best practice* operating and maintenance procedures will evolve. These practices need to be documented. It will quickly become daily routine to track information such as equipment histories, parts and materials, individual training progression, and costs. A well-chosen data management system will be an indispensable tool.

Systematic maintenance management requires the most effective way to reduce or mitigate the risk of failure. First, the nature of failure in a specific case must be understood. Then the remedy can be chosen, whether it be based on time, use or condition factors, or some other tactic.

Measurement

With continuous improvement, the current reality is judged against a future vision. In maintenance management, the prime objective is asset productivity: asset output divided by all inputs.

For TPM, it is also useful to measure continuous improvement success, including the number of active teams and their individual and collective progress. From the beginning, spreading the good news about progress beyond the shop floor will motivate everyone in the organization.

The future vision is best tempered with an understanding of what the competition, industry at large, or best-in-class have achieved. Benchmarking, described in Chapter 5, is useful in this regard.

Continuous Improvement Teams

Continuous improvement, based on *Kaizen* principles in Japan, is central to TQM and JIT. Organizations that have begun implementing TQM, JIT, or Continuous Improvement (CI) processes will have CI teams in place.

TPM teams tend to base their agenda on effective maintenance information management systems (for example, equipment histories for failure analysis). This begins with a Pareto review of failure of the equipment or processes that govern bottlenecking or add the most value to the product flow.

Operators in TPM build a strong relationship with their equipment. They drive an understanding within teams of failure causes, effects and impacts, and the resulting actions to eliminate these failures.

Processes

TPM is often a radical change in the way asset maintenance is managed. Some of the traditional processes for preventive, corrective, or breakdown maintenance and for stores inventory control are simply no longer appropriate.

In the new climate of responsiveness, flexibility, and empowerment, the existing processes must be revisited. They must be clearly understood, analyzed, and then redesigned to support the TPM objectives. Each step along the way must add value and minimize any waste in cost, time, service, quality, or other resources.

IMPLEMENTING TPM: THE ELEMENTS

What TPM means, and what it will accomplish, is different for each application. The implementation plan, too, needs to be specific to the situation and plant environment. A small woodworking firm with a tradition of production-maintenance integration could take a more informal approach than, say, a large, integrated steel mill. A basic methodology that has proved successful as a guide in many diverse applications is presented in Figure 8-2.

Following an implementation plan adapted from the Japan Institute of Plant Maintenance, the enterprise should progress through four phases in charting its new course. This route, which is described in more detail in *Training for TPM*, (Productivity Press, 1990), and in *TPM Development Program* (Productivity Press, 1989), progresses from stabilizing the mean time between failures and extending equipment life to predicting equipment life through condition monitoring. The four phases of activities are conducted by teams of production, maintenance, and engineering personnel working in concert. The entire implementation process is supported throughout by comprehensive education and training. (See Figure 8-3.)

Awareness, Education, and Training

Learning underscores each element of TPM. At Nachi-Fujikoshi Corporation in Japan, "Cultivating equipment-conscious workers is the base upon which every other feature of

	I. Stabilize Mean Time Between Failures	II. Lengthen Equipment Life	III. Periodically Restore Deterioration	IV. Predict Equipment Life
Autonomous (Operator) Maintenance	Restore accelerated deterioration by cleaning, lubricating and tightening, and correcting visible defects	Learn more about equipment mechanisms and functions; develop inspection skills	Conduct autonomous inspections and adjustments; organize and visually manage work areas	Manage operations and daily equipment care and inspections autonomously; carry out simple repairs and replacements
Equipment Improvement	Prevent accelerated deterioration with improvements to: • Control contamination sources • Enhance accessibility for cleaning, lube, and inspection Address chronic equipment losses and prevent recurrence	• Correct design and fabrication weaknesses • Prevent operating and repair errors • Eliminate sporadic failures • Improve maintainability and operability		• Further extend life using new materials and technologies • Learn and apply advanced failure analysis techniques
Planned Maintenance	• Prepare equipment logs • Help operators establish daily inspection and lubrication standards • Introduce visual controls • Clarify operating conditions; comply with conditions of use	• Rank failures, prioritize PM work • Standardize routine maintenance activities • Create data management systems to monitor failures, equipment, spares, costs	• Estimate life spans and learn early signs of internal deterioration • Set standards for periodic inspection and parts replacement • Improve efficiency of planned inspection and maintenance work and improve control of data and spares	• Apply condition-based monitoring techniques to predict life • Conduct periodic restoration based on predicted life
Quality Maintenance	Clarity relationship between quality and equipment, people, materials, methods		Establish and maintain equipment control conditions	
Maintenance Prevention	Define data system requirements and begin documenting equipment improvements	Incorporate data from current equipment improvements in new equipment design specifications		• Build in QM controls at the design stage

Source: Connie Dyer, Productivity, Inc.

Figure 8-2. TPM Implementation

	General Management	Maintenance Engineering	Operations	Maintenance
TPM objectives, elements, themes	✓	✓	✓	✓
General equipment cleaning, inspection, monitoring			✓	✓
Problem identification, analysis tools		✓	✓	✓
Basic equipment functioning, adjustment, optimization of skills			✓	✓
Focused technical skills				✓
Maintenance prevention and equipment redesign		✓	✓	✓

Figure 8-3. TPM Education and Training

[TPM] rests. Education and training is not only one of the fundamental improvement activities of TPM, it is a central pillar that supports the others."[*] Managers, maintenance staff, team leaders, and equipment operators all must be extensively involved in the learning process.

Training supports:

- *Decentralization* of decision-making and empowerment of employees. This will help them act autonomously, with knowledge and confidence, and as team players who know where and when to ask for help.
- *Maintenance prevention*, or minimizing the amount of maintenance intervention without sacrificing reliability. This is accomplished with standard operating procedures and systematic analysis and treatment of equipment failures and other abnormalities.

---

[*] Nachi-Fujikoshi Corporation, eds., *Training for TPM: A Manufacturing Success Story* (Productivity Press, 1990), 217.

- *Multi-skilling* to maximize flexibility, efficiency, and job satisfaction for both maintenance and production workers.
- *Performance measures* to assess the costs/benefits of TPM. Successes in the program are publicized, and shortcuts to achieving resource productivity are abandoned.

The use of tools and techniques for problem identification, definition, solution, and team decisionmaking are shown in Figure 8-4. These aids are invaluable for the learning process.

Beyond understanding the theory behind TPM, you must have some practical knowledge before making sweeping changes to the system. A pilot project in an area of the plant will work out any kinks and build experience and confidence in your implementation team.

Of great help in a trial run is a detailed before-after study. One effective method is to have staff photograph or videotape

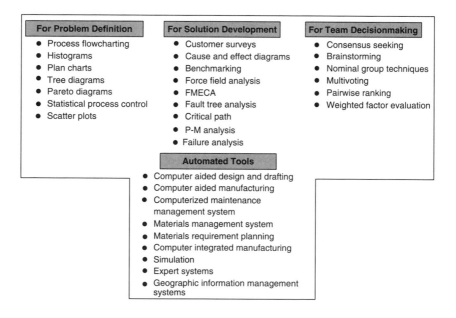

Figure 8-4. Tools and Techniques for TPM

the area, looking for defects, disorders, and deterioration. Such varied industries as aluminum rolling, primary steel, and discrete manufacturing have found that a series of pictures is, indeed, worth countless words of description. Keeping a visual record is part of the following eight-step approach for piloting:

1. *Education (basics)* — Companywide seminar on the elements, themes, and objectives of TPM, and how it relates to TQM, JIT, and CI programs that are already in place.
2. *Survey* — Determine which areas are likely to excel in a pilot program because of culture, attitude, preparation, or management style.
3. *Selection* — Select the pilot area based on its probability of success and on the productivity improvement potential. It should also be widely applicable to other areas of the operation.
4. *Data collection* — Carry out Pareto analyses of the frequency and duration of losses caused by recorded failures, setups, idling, minor delays, quality, and yield losses.
5. *Education (specifics)* — Present a detailed seminar for pilot area personnel describing the selection process, data analysis for equipment losses, and TPM vision.
6. *Photographic tour* — Have pilot teams take "as-is" photographs or videos of equipment deterioration, defects, disorders, housekeeping, and so on, in their area.
7. *Training* — Relate the Pareto analysis of losses to the results of the photographic tour. Also, provide training to minimize equipment deterioration and, therefore, equipment losses through the activities in Phase I — Stabilize Reliability
8. *Kickoff* — Choose a formal kickoff date and location for Phase I. Categorize responsibilities for improvement for production, materials, maintenance, and engineering.

It is critical to measure the progress of the pilot program to gain momentum for plantwide success. Monitor such "outputs" as:

- *Equipment effectiveness* — the product of availability, process rate, and quality rate.
- *Reliability* — mean time between failures.
- *Maintainability* — mean time to inspect, service, replace, or repair.

Also measure input such as

- *Labor*, including degree of PM compliance, demonstrated proficiency in autonomous maintenance, crew size, and maintenance labor distribution.
- *Materials*, including engineering stores inventory turns, inventory service level, vendor partnering, and obsolescence.
- *Cost effectiveness*, where costs are measured by function, area, equipment, job, and class of expense.

KEY SUCCESS FACTORS

The single most important factor to implement TPM is true management commitment. Organizations with this level of commitment are successful, even if they do not have the most comprehensive plan or a lavish budget. What does honest commitment mean? You could say it's a little like bacon and eggs — the chicken was involved, but the pig was committed!

Management's commitment is certainly shown by what it's willing to put on the line. The resources allocated are important, of course. But what counts even more are the time and visible involvement of senior management, for however long it takes to put TPM into place. Other key success factors include:

- The team approach throughout the project cycle.
- The enthusiasm and team-building skills of TPM leaders or project managers.
- A clearly defined methodology.
- The learning processes, particularly the communication between maintenance and operations in such vital areas

as *how* the equipment does what it does and *how to* keep it operating effectively.

- The mechanisms in place to reinforce positive behavior and results.

Many of North America's important manufacturers and processors are now fully immersed in TPM. Dupont Fibers attributes major gains in productive capacity to TPM: having skilled people getting their equipment up to as-new condition and keeping it there, and eliminating failures through systematic improvement over the long term. Others include Timkin, Pepsi, Ford, Harley-Davidson, Wilson Sporting, MACI, Saturn Corp., Norton, John Deere, Unilever, Steelcase, and, of course, Toyota. But as Mark O'Brien of Yamaha said, "As we looked around Japan and the U.S. for the perfect TPM recipe, we realized that no one has the cookbook."

A successful implementation of TPM themes and elements certainly results in measurable benefits. Empowered, motivated employees will contribute in significant ways to help improve asset productivity. The long-term benefit of caring about maintenance can be summed up in another quote from Pirsig:

> Each machine has its own personality, that is the real object of motorcycle maintenance. The new [machines] start out as good-looking strangers and, depending on how they are treated, degenerate rapidly into bad-acting grouches or even cripples, or else turn into healthy, good-natured, long lasting friends. This one, despite the murderous treatment it got at the hands of those alleged mechanics, seems to have recovered and has been requiring fewer repairs as time goes on. (*Zen and the Art of Motorcycle Maintenance, p. 39*)

Part IV

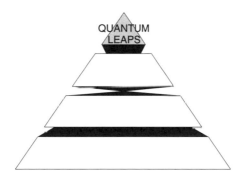

9

Reengineering Maintenance Processes

"Continuous improvement is exactly the right idea if you are the world leader in everything you do. It is a terrible idea if you are lagging in the world leadership benchmark. It is probably a disastrous idea if you are far behind the world standard. We need rapid, quantum leap improvement."

Paul O'Neill
Chairman, ALCOA

Process reengineering was first discussed in Michael Hammer's *Harvard Business Review* article, "Don't Automate, Obliterate." It is no less than a fundamental rethinking and radical redesign of business processes. The goal is to achieve dramatic performance advances in critical areas such as cost, quality, service, and speed. Instead of fine-tuning the status quo with continuous incremental improvement, reengineering focuses on core business processes, such as new product development, order fulfillment, and maintenance management. It zeros in on those that are crucial to success because they increase customer and shareholder value. (See Figure 9-1.)

MAINTENANCE: A PROCESS OR A FUNCTION

The first step in reengineering maintenance management is to stop thinking of it as a function, a discipline, a professional "silo." Maintenance management begins with a need, often expressed by a "customer," and ends with it being satisfied. The maintenance *process* is what makes it possible.

The problem with the functional view is that it makes you optimize the function and not the overall process. Maintenance

141

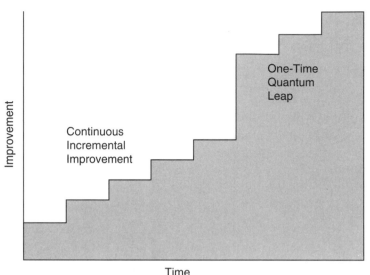

Figure 9-1. Quantum Leaps in Improvement

as a function usually covers only the trades. As a process, it covers trades, but also purchasing, stores, production scheduling, operations, engineering, and several other management and administrative functions.

One example of the problem of maintenance as a function is maintenance stores. Each silo has its own agenda to optimize performance:

- *Maintenance* — Because it is responsible for equipment availability, maintenance does not want to be caught without any part on hand to respond to breakdowns. It minimizes these failures by scheduling time for PMs and component replacements. Maximizing inventory optimizes its performance as a function, and open stores access across all shifts is preferable.
- *Production* — Its mandate is to produce during scheduled runs, so it does not want any equipment delays, not even for scheduled component replacements. Production

is usually measured on income statement accounts and is not concerned with balance sheet accounts, such as stores inventory.

- *Materials* — Minimizing freight charges and personnel costs dictates slow logistics and single-shift coverage for stores. Also, maximizing space and orderliness makes the function run smoothly. Day-shift, controlled access ensures minimal discrepancies in inventory reconciliation. The prime driver for this function is control, not necessarily service.
- *Finance* — Concerned with controlling the balance sheet, it therefore likes to minimize stores investment and carrying costs, often to an arbitrary, fixed level.
- *Engineering* — As part of capital project planning, engineering sets rigorous specifications, and follows a conservative route to maximize reliability when planning capital and replacement spares.
- *Purchasing* — Going out for numerous quotes and taking the lowest cost, while meeting the minimum specifications, ensures that cost savings targets are met but adds excessive variation in spare parts.
- *Plant management* — Often with roots in production or engineering, cost-cutting measures tend to be aimed at support functions like maintenance and stores.

Too often, the various departments involved negotiate an uneasy balance that favors one or two of them. The solution, of course, is to view equipment effectiveness and cost efficiency as results of the entire maintenance process. That depends on developing rational principles that get the most from all functions, not any particular one. If you can do that, maintenance process reengineering can improve your results radically.

BEGINNING REENGINEERING

To start, you must pull together a multidiscipline team from all the functions that make the process work. These include production, materials, engineering, maintenance and, in part, administration, depending on your organization structure. Then the techniques and tools should be chosen: at the very least, process mapping, process analysis, and customer interviews or surveys. You could also include automated tools to simulate how the reengineered process will work, and benchmarking to help set goals and provide insights. The team must clearly understand the overall vision of the business and what drives competitive advantage in your particular sector.

Next, map out the main working elements, such as how maintenance links or interfaces with other core processes, like production and engineering. Broad, aggressive goals — to achieve zero breakdowns in scheduled runs within 36 months, for instance — are defined at this point. Such visionary goals are unrealistic without the following expectations:

- There will be a major restructuring — in the way you are organized, the roles each person will play, the skills required, the way you are evaluated, the supporting technology, indeed, in the company culture.
- The top executive will commit an enormous amount of time at the site sponsoring and supporting the effort.
- There will be constant communication about the effort and progress that relate directly to profitability.

ANALYZING MAINTENANCE PROCESS FLOW

A process is a set of linked activities that take an input and transform it into an output. In maintenance, inputs involve identifying an equipment need and various materials, skills, and information. The linked activities include planning, scheduling, and the actual work. Outputs are available equipment, histories, and satisfied customers.

To reengineer maintenance, you need to understand clearly how the current process is actually conducted. Your objective is to simplify it to reduce cycle times, work-in-process, waste, and duplication.

Process Mapping

A straightforward, activity-based mapping technique using block diagrams is usually quite sufficient, except for complex processes, say, the in-situ rebuild of a major equipment system. Use a hierarchy and you can map at different levels, as shown in Figure 9-2. The first level may be the planned maintenance process. Level 2 delineates planned maintenance into the steps: notify, prepare, fix and review. Levels 3 and 4 breaks down these steps further. At the finest level of detail, you can pinpoint where improvement is needed most, because of high cost, long cycle time, frequency, quality problems, or overall impact on the entire process.

In mapping, you need to define the boundaries of the process, the beginning and end. The same is true for each activity within that process, and also who is the one actually doing the activity.

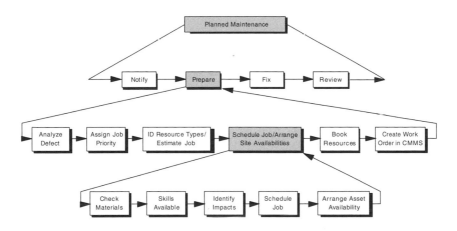

Figure 9-2. Process Flow Mapping

Process Analysis

For each activity, you need to know what is being done, how it is done, why it is done, what the volume is, who is involved, how long it takes, and what it costs. You must be able to answer the question, "Does this activity add value?" In other words, would customers pay for it if they knew you were doing it?

List which activities don't add value: move, inspect, file, store, retrieve, count, travel, wait. They all can't be eliminated, but they are good places to start streamlining. Figure 9-3 shows how to begin the value test, using an emergency maintenance request as an example.

There are tests that can be applied to each process and activity to determine its value. Can bureaucracy be reduced to eliminate unnecessary communications? Are there excess moves, waiting, filing, or rework? Is there an easier, simpler,

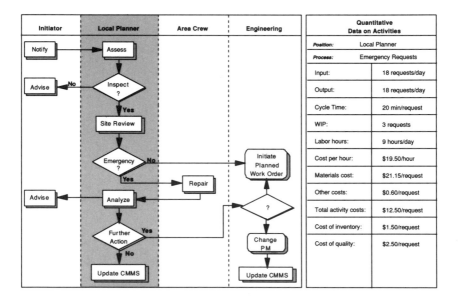

Figure 9-3. Process Analysis

or more streamlined approach, perhaps by changing the order, balancing tasks, or combining them? Duplication can often be eliminated by looking at redundancies or multiple versions. Often, you conduct activities in sequence when they can be done in parallel or along a critical path. When you look at the root cause of errors or quality problems, error-proofing is often a matter of standardization or using a specialist. Finally, automate the simple, repetitive tasks.

Visioning

Once the current process is understood in detail, you need an even more exact picture of what the reengineered model will look like. This is the core of the exercise, where you can easily get tripped up after all your careful planning. If you're lucky, said one frustrated maintenance manager, "then a miracle occurs." There is a series of creative and innovative tools to make this "miracle" happen:

- Ask the basic, hard questions, such as, "Why do we maintain our own equipment?" or "Do time-based PMs actually reduce our failure rates?"
- Brainstorm, use cause-effect diagrams, ask the "Five Why's," and use the tools of quality.
- Benchmark, particularly in businesses not related to your own but facing similar challenges.

Reengineering

The vision you build is the foundation of the reengineered process. The detailed plan, costs, and cycle times—these are the mechanics. Figure 9-4 shows how one company took out 21 steps and two positions in their corrective maintenance process.

Barriers to change and adjustments that must be made will soon become evident. The real issues will take shape as the

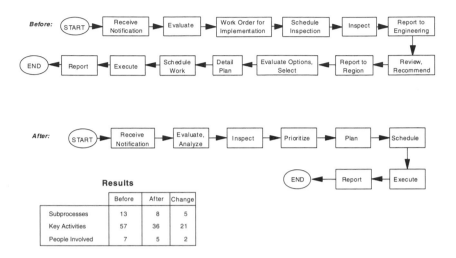

Figure 9-4. Simplifying the Corrective Maintenance Process

organization struggles to restructure. Supporting it all is senior executive leadership.

Management commitment to change cannot be stressed enough.

One utility company recently reorganized into business units, consolidating many of its maintenance specialists into a services unit. The makeover progressed rather smoothly. People were becoming comfortable with the change, when one of the managers introduced a maintenance process reengineering exercise for the civil works. The team took up this initiative with glee, producing celebratory results that were clearly superior to the status quo. Executive management cheered the reengineering exercise as a new approach to cost-effectiveness. But it wasn't prepared to implement the result, which basically contradicted the earlier maintenance centralization effort. Everyone went back to their familiar ways.

Reengineering is radical and dramatic. It can provide gigantic leaps in contemporary measures of performance. And it can also shake your operation to its roots. It is not for the faint-hearted.

10

Maintenance 2000

"When you aim for perfection, you discover it's a moving target."
George Fisher

Maintenance management has gone through some amazing changes this century. And so has the equipment — the physical resources used to manufacture, process, transport, and serve.

Trying to predict the future based on the past is dubious, at best. Just because it may take you an extra hour to reach your destination if one engine of the plane fails, it doesn't mean you'll be two hours late if both fail! However, equipment design and use are changing, and so must maintenance to keep pace.

CHANGING ASSETS — CHANGING TACTICS

In the first part of this century, machines were relatively simple, sturdy, and long-lasting. When the main moving parts or parts that came into contact with the product wore out, they would be rebuilt. Today, equipment is typically a complex hybrid of electromechanical devices; electronically controlled; with hydraulic, optic, or pneumatic subsystems (see Figure 10-1). It is characterized by replaceable components on a base structure. Because of its complexity and precision standards, failure patterns are somewhat random. Often, it is built to last for a predetermined use, to balance capital, operating, and disposal costs.

149

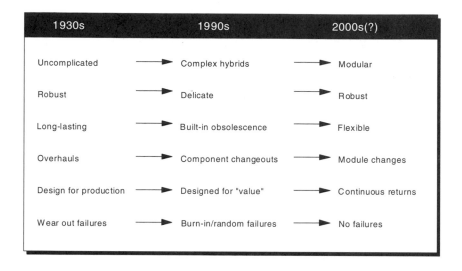

Figure 10-1. Changing Equipment Characteristics

In the next 25 years, you can reasonably expect equipment to become even more modular and automated to increase its operating flexibility. With continued marketplace globalization and competitive pressures, it must be both highly precise as well as robust. The failure rate will likely mimic that of complex equipment systems, but there will be an even stronger need for predictable performance. You'll need on-line condition monitoring, exacting diagnostics, and lightening-fast response.

An example is the automobile, which has changed tremendously over the past sixty years. The major oil companies are closing most service stations because there is so little demand for car repairs, despite major increases in the number of automobiles on the road. They just don't need as much maintenance because it has been engineered out. The new top-line cars have on-board diagnostics that rival those in jet aircraft.

What does this mean for maintenance management? If you look to the past for guidance, an interesting picture emerges. Figure 10-2 shows that the first generation of maintenance management had a strategy of run-to-failure. Specialist craft

Generation	1st	2nd	3rd	4th(?)
Strategy	**Breakdown**	**Prevention**	**Prediction**	**Reliance**
Structure	• Central craft groups	• Multicraft teams	• Multiskilled trades	• Polyskilled technician
Failure Management	• Operate to failure	• Scheduled overhaul	• FMECA and CBM	• Self-analysis
Data Management	• Card files	• Mainframe functions	• Fully functional CMMS	• Fully networked Stations
Measures	• Throughput	• Availability	• Equipment Effectiveness	• Probabilities

Figure 10-2. Maintenance Management Generations

groups—welders, electricians, riggers, etc.—were centrally dispatched to repair failures as they occurred.

After World War II, some emphasis was placed on basic lubrication and inspection, which grew into broad failure prevention programs such as plant shutdowns for maintenance, scheduled overhauls, and replacements. With competent tradespeople, the issue became one of coordinating these specialist crafts, not their technical supervision. Large computers came into use in most large enterprises, and some maintenance functions were automated, notably stores inventory control and PM scheduling.

Today, there is great interest in predictive maintenance—using condition-based monitoring to warn of impending failure, and analytical tools such as failure mode effect and criticality analysis (FMECA). With the advent of microcomputers and inexpensive packaged CMMS, information is much easier to store, manipulate, and review. Businesses now also want more from their equipment: the ability to produce high-quality products, at minimum cycle times.

The watchwords in the future will likely be *flexibility* and *reliability*. You'll need to clearly understand dominant failure mechanisms, to know instantaneous performance. If something does go wrong, you must have immediate expert advice on how to fix it.

In Chapter 4, you saw some basic condition-monitoring options. These will become broader in scope and more comprehensive to match increased equipment performance demands. The higher operating temperatures, pressures, speeds, and uptime for round-the-clock production dictate increased CBM. The interpretation of this information — the fault diagnosis and repair advice — is a little more challenging.

EXPERT SYSTEMS

It takes a real expert to understand problems in complex equipment today. Often, it takes a team of specialists when it comes to the most complex equipment systems — such as those in the aerospace, telecommunications, and nuclear fields. These experts will use all information on hand, not just data from CBM sensors. They review data from equipment histories and manufacturing design and information from similar equipment in like environments. They also use their personal wealth of experience, which is essential to interpret all this data, from all these sources.

Today, leading-edge maintenance management diagnostics include:

- Condition monitoring using vibration, lubrication, and thermographic analysis for generating data.
- CMMS for pulling all the data together.
- An expert system applied to one of the condition-monitoring techniques to recommend ways to diagnose the input data.

Expert systems have been developed to capture an individual's expertise. Simply put, these systems operate under a set of rules. They ask, you answer, and they lead you to the root cause of a symptom. For example, spectrographic oil analysis data for wear debris, additives, and contaminants, combined with data on viscosity and dilution, can be entered into a database. The expert system has a resident knowledge base built by people who understand the engine design and operation and the failure mechanisms. It also has a set of rules to decide what to do with the oil data, given the knowledge base. (See Figure 10-3.)

Research is now being conducted on expert systems that can do even more. For example, they can deal with situations beyond those covered by a strict set of rules for an equipment model. They have both a broader and deeper knowledge database. They learn from experience. The more sophisticated the expert system, the broader the range of equipment it can help, and the less specialized the system operator must be.

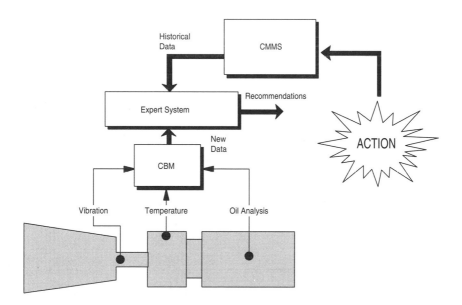

Figure 10-3. Expert System Data Flow

THE COMPLETE TECHNICIAN

What you are likely to see is more self-analysis built into equipment and less reliance on individual experts within each maintenance area, and a much greater capability of expert systems to provide the reliability needed. The maintenance technician will be multi-skilled within the crafts and cross-skilled with the operating personnel. Several companies have already started down this avenue, but it may take a generation of workers to see it through. New hires are selected on their ability to learn, personality traits such as self-esteem and confidence, and how they integrate into a team environment. They may have some trade or engineering skills to start; even so, they follow trade and operator training. They will be groomed to manage all aspects of an operation process and the tasks recommended by the expert systems for both maintenance and operations.

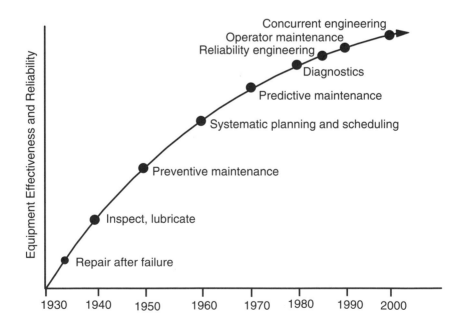

Figure 10-4. Emerging Strategies for Maintenance Management

Maintenance management is rapidly becoming an engineering specialty, like civil, mechanical, metallurgical, and electrical engineering. Several universities now offer undergraduate and postgraduate courses in maintenance engineering. Many emphasize a life-cycle approach to physical asset management: getting the people responsible for operating and maintaining the equipment involved in its design, manufacture, installation, and modification.

The performance of any machine is largely inherent in the design. Therefore, it will become more common to see the roles blurred between those who design and those who maintain.

EMERGING STRATEGIES

So what will be the definitive maintenance management strategy of the twenty-first century? Figure 10-4 shows the trend away from simple repair after failure to complex blends of engineering and the human element. One thing is certain. The sophistication and complexity of how the equipment is made and what it can do must be matched by the same level of expertise in maintenance strategy and tactics.

Bibliography

Cooksey, et al. *Process Improvement — A Guide for Teams*. Arlington, Va.: Coopers & Lybrand, 1993.

Cross, H. *Changing Job Structures*, London: Heinemann Newnes, 1990.

Hammer, M., and J. Champy. *Re-engineering the Corporation*. New York: Harper Business, 1993.

Hoenslaar, W.J.A. *Maintenance for the 1990s*. IISI, 1989.

Johansson, et al. *Business Process Re-engineering*. New York: John Wiley, 1993.

Kelly, A. *Maintenance and Its Management*. Farnham, Surrey, U.K.: Conference Communication, 1989.

McNair, D.J., and K.H.J. Liebfried. *Benchmarking: A Tool for Continuous Improvement*. New York: Harper Business, 1992.

Moubray, J.M. *Reliability-Centred Maintenance*. Oxford, U.K.: Butterworth Heinemann, 1991.

Nachi-Fujikoshi Corp., ed. *Training for TPM*. Portland, Ore.: Productivity Press, 1990.

Nakajima, S. *TPM Development Program*. Portland, Ore.: Productivity Press, 1989.

Pirsig, Robert M. *Zen and the Art of Motorcycle Maintenance*. New York: Bantam Books, 1974, pp. 9, 25, 39.

Salee, A.M. *CMMS User Handbook*. New York: Thomas Marketing, 1993.

Suzuki, T. *New Directions for TPM*. Portland, Ore.: Productivity Press, 1992.

Wireman, T. *Computerized Maintenance Management Systems*. New York: Industrial Press, 1986.

Appendix A

The Maintenance Management Diagnostic Review

Key Areas for Assessment

I. Characteristics of the Business
    - Plant layout, facilities, fleet sizes, and makeup; age
    - Process flow and technology; equipment criticality
    - Organization structure and labor levels
    - Business plan and competitive dimensions; nature of cycle
    - Operating policies, plans, and schedules; shutdown windows
    - Special regulatory, environmental, safety considerations

II. Maintenance Strategy
    - Documented mandate, principles, objectives, and improvement plan
    - Degree of fit with business characteristics
    - Overview of plant, facility, fleet condition; housekeeping
    - Capital expenditure history; upgrading of plant

- Overall maintenance budget over past several years
- Use of contractors, partnering

III. Organizational Arrangements
- Structure, preferred communication channels, logical groupings
- Number of personnel by craft, trade, function
- Existence of maintenance planning, maintenance engineering
- Key accountabilities of each position; overlaps, gaps
- Degree of autonomy, self-direction, teamwork
- Links with materials management, administrative systems, etc.
- Appropriate location of maintenance personnel
- Organization level of maintenance management
- Communication preferences: direction, consultation, facilitation

IV. Human Resource Management
- Morale, absenteeism, turnover, grievance level
- Suggestion plans, continuous improvement teams
- Compensation system, incentives, recognition, rewards
- Overall working conditions, degree of satisfaction, labor relations
- Training processes: technical, general, supervisory, problem solving, teamwork, maintenance management
- Safety record, loss prevention, analysis and correction, discipline, participation
- Personnel performance evaluation, employee development, career progression; selection of new employees

V. Maintenance Administration
- The annual budgeting process and involvement

- Cost reporting, availability of information, cost control
- Data collection, data entry, integration
- Records management for personnel, equipment, costing
- Drawings for layout, equipment configuration, updating, control

VI.   Planning
- Responsibilities for fault identification, general work identification
- Priority setting, collaboration; scoping the work
- Planning of activities, sequencing, coordination of skills, estimating
- Scoping for parts, components, materials; cost allocation
- Special tools, mobile equipment, rigging, preliminary shopwork
- Reference drawings, safety reminders
- External contractor arrangements, special orders
- Use of standard procedures for repetitive work

VII. Scheduling
- Backlog of special work, preventive maintenance, shutdowns
- Coordination with production, stores; daily, weekly meetings
- Net capacity review for special skills
- Scheduling horizons for production planning, labor balancing
- Use of decision support tools, large job scheduling techniques

VIII. Work Orders
- Various types: PM, lubrication, corrective, urgent, standing
- Authorization levels and procedures, costing technique

- Use of work orders: costs, records, productivity, failure analysis, job plans, backlogs, scheduling
- Automated or paper driven
- Originator, planner, scheduler, doer, analyzer, recorder
- Feedback provided on actual vs. planned
- Use of data, notifications

IX. Use of Tactics
- Level of unplanned, urgent, emergency, standing work orders
- Level of planned, preventive, predictive scheduled maintenance
- Degree of compliance with planned work schedules
- Quality control and management on maintenance activities and schedules
- Coverage of equipment, areas for planned maintenance
- Level of detail on preventive, predictive maintenance routines
- Work generated as a result of inspections
- Use of condition-based and nondestructive techniques
- Use of equipment histories for fault/failure analysis
- Documentation of downtime, causes, corrective action, inspection schedules

X. Equipment Records
- Analysis of critical equipment, configuration management, asset lists
- Nameplate, procurement information with bill of materials
- Histories of faults, failures, causes, repairs, actions, costs, times
- Functional standards for operation
- Assets clearly marked, nameplated
- Records management for manuals, drawings

- Access to records, use of records for prediction, problem solving, capital replacement, life-cycle management

XI. Purchasing
- Clear policies, procedures, accountabilities
- Vendor qualification; performance monitoring on cost, accuracy, quality, service, stability
- Vendor partnering, systems contracts, cooperative negotiations
- Approval process, levels for purchase requisitioning
- Coordination with maintenance on specifications, quality, service
- Level of urgent, emergency requisitions from maintenance
- Purchasing performance monitoring re-cost, customer satisfaction
- Expediting procedure
- Administrative processes for procurement, accounts payable
- Warranty management procedures, discrepancies
- Use of purchasing for obsolescence, engineering changes, new item testing

XII. Stores
- Layout, locations, access, space, racking, security
- Equipment, mobile equipment
- Degree of automation, bar coding
- Substores, shop-floor stores, free access items
- Receiving, issuing, stocking schedules, labor, procedures
- Direct charge item storage
- Quality assurance, accuracy
- Telephone orders, delivery, kitting/pick lists
- Consignment stock locations, vendor access
- Requisitioning procedures

XIII.   Inventory Control
- Catalogs, referencing, on-line information
- Inventory reconciliation and absolute value of deviation
- Use of statistical analysis by inventory category, stock history
- Measures of investment efficiency, turnover, value, number of SKUs
- Obsolescence review, no usage analysis
- Stock control techniques, max-min, EOQ, EOP
- Control of repairables, rotables
- Service level/stockout measures, back orders
- Stock counting policies, schedules

XIV.   Performance Measures
- Cost breakdown by area, cost center, responsibility center, equipment/main components, work order, work category, type of expense (labor, material, overhead, etc.)
- Equipment performance for frequency and duration of failure, speed, precision, availability, utilization, reliability
- Process performance such as work orders by status, PM compliance, time on planned work, backlog, new tactics applied
- Employee performance, specialty training taken, application of skills, teamwork, progression

XV.   Customer Satisfaction
- Response time to urgent calls, flexibility, coverage
- Quality of work and call backs
- Housekeeping after repairs
- Schedule compliance and notification
- Level of confidence in maintenance by production
- Costs, estimates, and budget control

- Common goals, objectives, customer orientation, process orientation

XVI.   Computerized Maintenance Management Systems
- In place or planned
- Degree of use and coverage
- Capability of modules, functions
- Integration with other systems
- Used by shop-floor personnel; user friendliness

Appendix B

Computerized Maintenance
Management Systems Software
Characteristics Matrix

CLIENT'S RATE	PACKAGE RATE		PAGE
0	0	SECTION I EQUIPMENT FILES	
0	0	SECTION II WORK ORDER MANAGEMENT	
0	0	SECTION III PREVENTIVE MAINTENANCE	
0	0	SECTION IV PARTS & INVENTORY	
0	0	SECTION V PURCHASING	
0	0	SECTION VI FINANCIAL	
0	0	SECTION VII PERSONNEL	
0	0	SECTION VIII PACKAGE DOCUMENTAION	
0	0	SECTION IX HARDWARE PLATFORMS	
0	0	SECTION X SYSTEM REQUIREMENTS	
0	0	TOTALS	

SECTION I—EQUIPMENT FILES

PACKAGE RATING

1 INPUT OF EQUIPMENT IDENTIFICATION (MIN 20 POS.) _____
2 MULTIPLE TEXT LINES OF DESCRIPTION FOR EACH EQUIPMENT _____
3 NUMBER OF LEVELS OF STRUCTURE IN EQUIPMENT BOM (MIN 5) _____
4 ON-LINE TOP DOWN VIEW OF EQUIPMENT STRUCTURE _____
5 ON-LINE ON-SITE VIEW OF EQUIPMENT PARTS _____
6 MULTIPLE TEXT LINES OF DESCRIPTION FOR EACH PART OF EQUIPMENT _____
7 INPUT OF EQUIPMENT SUPPLIER _____
8 INPUT OF LOCATION (BUILDING, DEPARTMENT, ETC.) OF EQUIPMENT _____
9 DATE WHEN EQUIPMENT INSTALLED _____
10 SUPPLIER OF EQUIPMENT _____
11 PURCHASE PRICE & DATE PURCHASED _____
12 LINK TO STANDARD MAINTENANCE TASK ROUTINGS _____
13 DISPLAY OF SPARE PARTS FOR THAT (PART OF) EQUIPMENT _____
14 SELECTION FROM DISPLAY SPARE PARTS FOR INSERTING TO WO _____

		PACKAGE RATING
1	MAINTENANCE HISTORY FOR EACH EQUIPMENT AND EQUIPMENT PART	_____
2	HISTORY FOR EACH EQUIPMENT AND EQUIPMENT PART ON-LINE	_____
3	FOR EACH EQUIPMENT AND EQUIPMENT PART STANDARD HISTORY REPORTS	_____
4	DISPLAY OF PAST MAINTENANCE JOBS ON EQUIPMENT AND PARTS OF EQUIPMENT	_____
5	MULTIPLE TEXT LINES PER REPORTED/CLOSED JOB OR TASK	_____
6	WHILE CLOSING A WORK ORDER INPUT OF THE CIRCUMSTANCES	_____
7	AUTOMATICALLY CALCULATED DOWNTIME CAN BE MANUALLY OVERRIDDEN	_____
8	DOWNTIME OF EQUIPMENT PER WORK ORDER	_____
9	DOWNTIME OF EQUIPMENT YEAR TO DATE, PREVIOUS YEAR, ETC.	_____
10	HOURS REPORTED TO WORK ORDERS AND COLLECTED BY:	_____
11	—PER EQUIPMENT AND EQUIPMENT PARTS	_____
12	—TOTALS THIS YEAR SEPARATED BY TRADES	_____
13	—TOTALS PREVIOUS YEAR SEPARATED BY TRADES	_____
14	—TOTALS PER DEPARTMENT (LOCATION)	_____
15	—TOTALS PER DEPARTMENT AND EQUIPMENT (COMPARISON)	_____

SECTION II—WORK ORDER MANAGEMENT

		PACKAGE RATING
1	ORDER STATUS: REQUEST	_____
2	ORDER STATUS: PREPARED/PLANNED	_____
3	ORDER STATUS: WAITING FOR MATERIALS	_____
4	ORDER STATUS: READY FOR RELEASE	_____
5	ORDER STATUS: RELEASED/OPEN (EQUIPMENT DOWN)	_____
6	ORDER STATUS: RELEASED/OPEN (EQUIPMENT RUNNING)	_____
7	ORDER STATUS: CLOSED	_____
8	WO STATUS SUMMARY REPORT	_____
9	AUTOMATIC WO NUMBERING	_____
10	AUTOMATIC/MANUAL WO NUMBERING MIXED ALLOWED	_____
11	AUTOMATIC WO GENERATION FROM PM SCHEDULING	_____
12	PM-WO GENERATION WITH ROUTING TASKS INSERTED	_____
13	WORK ORDER START DATE	_____
14	WORK ORDER END DATE	_____
15	WORK ORDER PREPARED BY	_____
16	WO TYPE (CORRECTIVE, MODIFICATION, PREVENTIVE, ETC.)	_____
17	MANUALLY UPDATE CALCULATED DOWNTIME HOURS	_____
18	STANDARD ROUTING AND/OR TASKS SELECTION	_____
19	ON-LINE UPDATES ROUTING/TASKS AFTER SELECTION	_____
20	ACTIVITIES SEQUENCING (NETWORK)	_____
21	BACKSCHEDULING FROM END DATE	_____
22	FOREWARD SCHEDULING FROM START DATE	_____
23	BACK/FORWARD SCHEDULING WITH QUEUE SQUEEZE	_____
24	ON-LINE CONFIRMATION REQUIRED AGAINST AVAILABLE CAPACITY	_____
25	ON-LINE UPDATES OF CAPACITY AVAILABILITY	_____
26	ON-LINE SIMULATION (WHAT IF)	_____
27	ON-LINE DAILY WORKLOAD REPORT (WORK ORDER SEQUENCE BY PRIORITY)	_____
28	ON-LINE SIMULATION OF SPARE PARTS AVAILABILITY	_____
29	ON-LINE ALLOCATION CAPABILITY OF SPARE PARTS NEEDED	_____
30	PICKLIST PREPARATION (SEPARATED FOR SEPARATED STORES)	_____
31	PICKLIST SEQUENCED WITH PICKING LOGIC	_____
32	PICKLIST LOGIC BY DELIVERY LOCATION/OPERATION	_____
33	SHOP TRAVELER PRINTED	_____
34	ON-LINE PICKLIST AND SHOP TRAVELER GENERATION	_____
35	PICKLIST AND SHOP TRAVELER BAR CODED	_____
36	ON-LINE CONFIRMATION OF PICK COMPLETE OR PARTIALLY PICKED	_____
37	ORDER RELEASE CAN BE FORCED MANUALLY	_____
38	ON-LINE WO INQUIRY	_____
39	ON-LINE SELECTION ON WORK ORDER STATUS	_____
40	ON-LINE WO INQUIRY BY EQUIPMENT OR EQUIPMENT PARTS	_____
41	ON-LINE WO INQUIRY ROUTING/TASKS	_____
42	TIME PHASED SPARE PARTS AVAILABILITY CHECK	_____
43	ON-LINE MONITORING AND CONTROL OF WORK ORDERS	_____
44	PROGRESS REPORT	_____

```
45  ON-LINE COMPLETION REPORTING BY OPERATIONS/TASKS            _____
46  PARTIAL COMPLETION REPORTING/INPUT OF REMAINING HOURS/DURATION _____
47  ON-LINE WO CLOSE                                            _____
48  PROJECT PLANNING FOR MULTIPLE WORK ORDERS                   _____
49  TRANSFER OF WORK ORDERS TO A PROJECT                        _____
50  ENTERING NEW ACTIVITIES/OPERATIONS FOR A PROJECT            _____
51  RELATIONS BETWEEN WORK ORDERS AND ACITIVITES (SEQUENCING)   _____
52  ADDING NEW ACTIVITIES AFFECTS THE SAME CAPACITY/RESOURCES AS WO'S _____
53  PROJECT PLANNING AND DECISION SUPPORT                       _____
54  EMERGENCY CALLS (WORK ORDERS) SUPPORTED                     _____
55  CRITICAL PATH SCHEDULING                                    _____
```

PACKAGE
RATING

```
 1  ON-LINE ADD/DELETE/UPDATE OF:                               _____
 2  —ROUTINGS/TASKS                                            _____
 3  —MACHINE OR LABOR HOURS PER TASK                           _____
 4  —MILTIPLE LINES OF DESCRIPTION PER OPERATION/TASK          _____
 5  —MULTIPLE USE OF TIME UNITS (HOURS AND MINUTES)            _____
 6  —POSTOPERATION/TRANSPORT TIME BETWEEN TWO OPERATIONS/TASKS  _____
 7  —OPERATION/TASK EFFECTIVITY DATING                         _____
 8  —SEPARATE MACHINE AND LABOR HOURS                          _____
 9  —NUMBER OF EMPLOYEES                                       _____
10  AUTOMATIC NUMBERING OPERATIONS/TASKS WITHIN A ROUTING       _____
11  COMBINING A ROUTING FROM STANDARD OPERATIONS/TASKS          _____
12  CREATION AND USE OF STANDARD ROUTINGS                       _____
13  OVERLAP OF OPERATIONS/TASKS (PARTLY PARALLEL)               _____
14  ON-LINE ADD/UPDATE OF SPARE PARTS NEEDED                    _____
15  COPY FACILITIES FROM OTHER WORK ORDERS                      _____
```

PACKAGE
RATING

```
 1  ON-LINE ADD/UPDATE OF RESOURCES (TOOLS, EQUIPMENT, CREWS, ETC.) _____
 2  CAPACITY VARIABLE PER RESOURCE BY TIME PERIOD               _____
 3  NUMBER OF EMPLOYEES OR CREW SIZE PER RESOURCE               _____
 4  EFFECTIVE PRODUCTION HOURS A DAY                            _____
 5  TIME UNITS OF RESOURCES IN HOURS                            _____
 6  TIME UNITS OF RESOURCES IN MINUTES                          _____
 7  COST RATES BY RESOURCE                                      _____
 8  AVAILABLE NUMBER OF EMPLOYEES IN A RESOURCE                 _____
 9  CAPACITY REPORT PER AVAILABLE RESOURCE                      _____
10  NUMBER OF SHIFTS PER DAY/RESOURCE                           _____
11  HORIZON AVAILABLE CAPACITY PER RESOURCE (>6 MONTHS)         _____
12  INTEGRATION OF CONTRACTORS AS RESOURCES                     _____
```

SECTION III—PREVENTIVE MAINTENANCE

PACKAGE
RATING

```
 1  NUMBER OF DIFFERENT INTERVALS PER EQUIPMENT                 _____
 2  NUMBER OF DIFFERENT INTERVALS PER PARTS OF EQUIPMENT        _____
 3  NUMBER OF DIFFERENT ROUTINGS PER INTERVAL/EQUIPMENT/PART OF EQUIPMENT _____
 4  PREVENTIVE MAINTENANCE SCHEDULING                          _____
 5  METHOD FOR PM SCHEDULING TIME-BASED INTERVAL                _____
 6  METHOD FOR PM SCHEDULING METER READING INTERVAL             _____
 7  METHOD FOR PM SCHEDULING CONDITION-BASED INTERVAL           _____
 8  METHODS FOR PM SCHEDULING CAN BE MIXED PER EQUIPMENT        _____
 9  ON-LINE INQUIRY OF PM ACTIONS PER EQUIPMENT OR PART OF EQUIPMENT _____
10  MANUALLY INPUT OF RESULT METER READING                      _____
11  TIME-BASED INTERVAL IN DAYS                                 _____
12  TIME-BASED INTERVAL IN WEEKS                                _____
13  TIME-BASED INTERVAL IN MONTHS                               _____
14  TIME-BASED INTERVAL IN QUARTERLY                            _____
15  ON-LINE SIMULATION (WHAT IF) OF PM SCHEDULE PER (PART) EQUIPMENT _____
16  ON-LINE CONFIRMATION AND UPDATING PM SCHEDULE               _____
```

SECTION IV—PARTS INVENTORY

		PACKAGE RATING
1	PART NUMBER >15 POSITIONS	_____
2	(ISSUE) UNIT OF MEASURES >1	_____
3	BOM CONVERSION FACTORS	_____
4	PART RESPONSIBILITIES	_____
5	TRANSACTION HISTORY ON-LINE BY PART	_____
6	TRANSACTION HISTORY REPORT	_____
7	DRAWING NUMBER	_____
8	PRIMARY (PREFERRED) VENDOR	_____
9	SUBSTITUTION PART NUMBER(S)	_____
10	ON-LINE PARTS UPDATES	_____
11	PART UPDATES REPORTS	_____
12	AD HOC REPORTS	_____
13	INVENTORY ACCOUNT NUMBER	_____
14	MULTIPLE LINES OF EXTENDED PART DESCRIPTION	_____
15	PART DESCRIPTION >30 POSITIONS	_____
16	PRIMARY WAREHOUSE AND/OR LOCATION	_____
17	PART TYPES (MANUFACTURING OF PURCHASE PART)	_____
18	INSPECTION CODE	_____
19	STOCKING POLICIES (STOCK, NONSTOCK, FLOOR STOCK)	_____
20	COST INFORMATION (CURRENT, ACTUAL)	_____
21	—MATERIAL	_____
22	—LABOR	_____
23	—OUTSIDE OPERATIONS	_____
24	—TOTAL COSTS	_____
25	PURCHASE LEAD TIMES (REQUISITIONING, VENDOR, RECEIVING)	_____
26	MANUFACTURING LEAD TIMES	_____
27	TAX CODE(S)	_____
28	ORDER QUANTITY POLICY: DISCRETE	_____
29	ORDER QUANTITY POLICY: EOQ	_____
30	ORDER QUANTITY POLICY: FIXED QUANTITY	_____
31	ORDER QUANTITY POLICY: MULTIPLES OF FIXED QUANTITIES	_____
32	ORDER QUANTITY POLICY: PERIOD ORDER QUANTITY	_____
33	SAFETY STOCK	_____
34	REORDER POLICY: REORDER POINT	_____
35	REORDER POLICY: TIME-PHASED REORDER POINT	_____
36	CALCULATES EOQ AND REPORTING	_____
37	ABC ANALYSIS AND REPORTING	_____
38	ON-HAND, ISSUES, RECEIPTS IN DECIMAL QUANTITIES	_____
39	INPUT OF SPECIFIC EQUIPMENT IDENTIFICATION NUMBER(S)	_____

		PACKAGE RATING
1	ON-LINE TRANSACTIONS FOR ISSUES AGAINST A WORK ORDER	_____
2	ON-LINE TRANSACTIONS FOR UNPLANNED ISSUES	_____
3	ON-LINE TRANSACTIONS FOR RECEIPTS ON PURCHASE ORDER	_____
4	ON-LINE TRANSACTIONS FOR UNPLANNED RECEIPTS	_____
5	ON-LINE TRANSACTIONS FOR WAREHOUSE/LOCATION TRANSFERS	_____
6	ON-LINE TRANSACTIONS FOR FOR ADJUSTMENTS	_____
7	ON-LINE TRANSACTIONS FOR WORK ORDER RETURNS	_____
8	ON-LINE TRANSACTIONS FOR HANDLING ROTABLES (REPAIRABLES):	_____
9	—ISSUES/RECEIPTS BY ''REPAIRED'' OR ''NOT YET'' REPAIRED	_____
10	—STOCK STATUS BY ''REPAIRED'' OR ''NOT'' REPAIRED	_____
11	STOCK STATUS DISPLAY OF REORDER POINT AND ALLOCATION	_____
12	STOCK STATUS BY ON-HAND, ALLOCATED, ON ORDER	_____
13	STOCK STATUS WITH REORDER POINT AND ACTION MESSAGES	_____
14	STOCK STATUS WITH OPEN ORDERS AND TIME-PHASED ALLOCATIONS	_____
15	SUMMARIZED PART ALLOCATIONS BY WAREHOUSE/LOCATION (BIN)	_____
16	ON-LINE ADD/UPDATE/DELETE OF INVENTORY LOCATIONS (BINS)	_____
17	PROVIDES CYCLE COUNTING METHOD	_____
18	ON-HAND BALANCES IN STORES BY RECEIVING/INSPECTION	_____
19	BAR CODE SUPPORT BY ISSUES AND RECEIPTS	_____
20	EMPTY BIN REPORT	_____

```
21  STOCK BELOW REORDER POINT REPORT                                    _____
22  STOCK BELOW SAFETY STOCK REPORT
                                                                        PACKAGE
                                                                        RATING
 1  ON-LINE PRINTING OF A RECEIVING TRAVELER                            _____
 2  ON-LINE PRINTING OF A BAR CODED RECEIVING TRAVELER                  _____
 3  ON-LINE DEBIT MEMO PRINTING BY RETURN TO VENDOR                     _____
 4  ON-LINE PO RECEIPT                                                  _____
 5  ON-LINE SUBCONTRACT ORDER RECEIPT                                   _____
 6  ON-LINE TRANSACTION FOR RETURN TO VENDOR                            _____
 7  ON-LINE TRANSACTION OF SCRAP                                        _____
 8  ON-LINE TRANSACTION TO INCOMING INSPECTION                          _____
 9  ON-LINE TRANSACTION FOR RECEIPTS TO STORES                          _____
10  ON-LINE TRANSACTION FOR REJECTING RECEIPTS                          _____
11  ON-LINE ISSUE TO WO FROM RECEIVING STAGE OR INSPECTION              _____
12  ON-LINE ADDING OF DISCREPANT DELIVERIES AND ACTION MESSAGES         _____
13  DOCK TO STOCK SUPPORT AND TRACKING                                  _____
14  RECEIVING INTEGRATED WITH PURCHASING                                _____
15  RECEIVING INTEGRATED WITH INVENTORY WAREHOUSE                       _____
16  DOCK TO STOCK AND TRACKING SUPPORT                                  _____
17  ON-LINE INFORMATION OF: ITEM DESCRIPTION                            _____
18       UNIT OF MEASURES                                               _____
19     —INSPECTION REQUIREMENTS                                         _____
20     —HANDLING INSTRUCTIONS                                           _____
21  UPDATING (ON-LINE) OF ORDER, ITEM, AND TRANSACTION HISTORY          _____
22  DAILY RECEIVING REPORT                                              _____

                        SECTION V—PURCHASING

                                                                        PACKAGE
                                                                        RATING
 1  PURCHASE ORDERS: STANDARD PURCHASE ORDER                            _____
 2  PURCHASE ORDERS: BLANKET/CONTRACT                                   _____
 3  PURCHASE ORDERS: SUBCONTRACT ORDER                                  _____
 4  PURCHASE ORDER STATUS: INCOMPLETE                                   _____
 5  PURCHASE ORDER STATUS: OPEN, PLACED                                 _____
 6  PURCHASE ORDER STATUS: CLOSED                                       _____
 7  REQUISITION STATUS: INCOMPLETE                                      _____
 8  REQUISITION STATUS: COMPLETE                                        _____
 9  REQUISITION STATUS: CLOSED                                          _____
10  PO/BLANKET ORDERS/SUBCONTRACT ORDERS CAN HAVE >1 ITEM/ORDERLINE     _____
11  PO ITEMS CAN CONTAIN MULTIPLE DELIVERIES PER ITEM/ORDERLINE         _____
12  PO CAN HANDLE PURCHASE UNIT OF MEASURES                             _____
13  REQUISITIONS CAN HANDLE PURCHASE UNIT OF MEASURES                   _____
14  COPY FACILITIES FOR PO'S                                            _____
15  COPY FACILITIES FOR REQUISITIONS                                    _____
16  GROUPING SEVERAL REQUISITIONS TO ONE PURCHASE ORDER                 _____
17  CREATE PURCHASE ORDER DIRECTLY WITHOUT REQUISITION                  _____
18  INTERFACE CAPABILITY REQUISITION TO AN EXISTING PO SYSTEM           _____
19  MANUAL AND AUTOMATIC WORK ORDER NUMBERING BOTH ALLOWED              _____
20  PO IN MULTIPLE LANGUAGES                                            _____
21  SUPPORTS MULTIPLE CURRENCY                                          _____
22  ON-LINE PO PRERELEASE REVIEW                                        _____
23  ON-LINE ACCESS TO PURCHASE PART HISTORY                             _____
24  PART PURCHASE HISTORY                                               _____
25  CONSIGNED MATERIAL SUPPORT INCLUDING PICKLIST                       _____
26  REVISION OF PURCHASE ORDERS (INCLUDING PRINTING) SUPPORTED          _____
27  ON-LINE QUOTATION ENTRY                                             _____
28  PRICE BREAKS IN QUOTATIONS SUPPORTED                                _____
29  MULTIPLE DISCOUNTS AND SUBCHARGES                                   _____
30  AUTOMATIC SUPPLIER SELECTION: PREFERRED SOURCE                      _____
31  AUTOMATIC SUPPLIER SELECTION: SUPPLIER BALANCE                      _____
32  AUTOMATIC SUPPLIER SELECTION: PRICE                                 _____
33  AUTOMATIC SUPPLIER SELECTION: LEAD TIME                             _____
34  PO FOLLOWS-UP TRIGGERS                                              _____
35  REQUISITIONS FOLLOW-UP TRIGGERS                                     _____
36  ACCEPT AND REWORK OPTIONS TO CLOSE AN ORDER                         _____
```

37	RETURN TO VENDOR OPTIONS	____
38	SUPPLIER QUOTATION FILE MAINTAINED WITH PURGE LOGIC	____
39	ON-LINE INQUIRY: ITEMS SUPPLIED BY VENDOR	____
40	MULTIPLE ADDRESSES PER VENDOR	____
41	VENDOR PART NUMBER(S) AND DESCRIPTION(S)	____
42	VENDOR LEAD-TIME CALCULATED MANUALLY OR AUTOMATIC	____
43	SUPPLIER PERFORMANCE SUPPORT	____
44	ON-LINE ENTRY AND UPDATE OF REQUISITIONS	____
45	PO HEADER MULTIPLE TEXTLINES	____
46	PO FOOTER MULTIPLE TEXTLINES	____
47	PO MULTIPLE DETAIL (ITEM OR ORDERLINE) TEXTLINES	____
48	PO STANDARD TEXT SUPPORT	____
49	PRINTING OF REMINDERS (EXPEDITING)	____
50	PRINTING OF REQUEST FOR QUOTATIONS	____
51	PART/ITEM PURCHASE REPORT	____
52	PART/SUPPLIER QUOTATIONS REPORT	____
53	REQUISITIONS REPORT	____
54	PO STATUS AND FOLLOW-UP REPORT	____
55	RELEASED PURCHASE ORDERS BY PART REPORT	____
56	PURCHASE ORDERS IN VENDORS SEQUENCE REPORT	____
57	PURCHASE ORDERS IN BUYER AND/OR EXPEDITOR SEQUENCE REPORT	____
58	VENDOR PERFORMANCE REPORT	____
59	VARIABLE PO PRINT LAYOUT	____
60	ON-LINE PRINTING OF PO'S	____
61	BATCH PRINTING OF PO'S	____

SECTION VI—FINANCIAL

PACKAGE
RATING

1	FINANCIAL OVERVIEW OF EACH EQUIPMENT SPEND/BUDGET	____
2	FINANCIAL OVERVIEW OF SPEND/BUDGET INCLUDING PREVIOUS YEAR(S)	____
3	FINANCIAL OVERVIEW OF SPEND/BUDGET BY DEPARTMENT	____
4	INPUT OF BUDGET AMOUNT FOR EACH EQUIPMENT	____
5	INPUT OF BUDGET AMOUNT FOR A PART OF EQUIPMENT	____
6	INPUT OF COSTS PER HOUR PER RESOURCE	____
7	INPUT OF ADDITIONAL COSTS BY CLOSING WORK ORDER	____
8	INPUT OF BUDGET AMOUNT (HRS) PER RESOURCE/WORK ORDER	____
9	TRIGGERING REPORTS WHEN BUDGET EQUALS SPEND	____
10	BUDGETING INTEGRATED WITH WORK ORDER/STORAGE/PURCHASING	____
11	VARIABLE INPUT OF BUDGET INTERVAL	____
12	REPORT OF COSTS DIVIDED IN LABOR, MATERIAL, PURCHASED AND ADDITIONAL	____
13	REPORT OF COST DIVIDED IN TYPE MAINTENANCE (PM, CORRECTIVE, ETC.)	____
14	TRACKING INFORMATION DOWN TO COMPONENT LEVEL	____

SECTION VII—PERSONNEL

PACKAGE
RATING

1	INPUT OF EMPLOYEES—NUMBER	____
2	INPUT EMPLOYEES NAME	____
3	INPUT OF EMPLOYEES RESOURCE GROUP, ASSIGNMENT AREA	____
4	VARIABLE HOURS TO BE REPORTED PER DAY/EMPLOYEE	____
5	VARIABLE INPUT OF SHIFTS PER DAY/EMPLOYEE	____
6	REPORTING HOURS AGAINST WORK ORDERS	____
7	NUMBER OF WORK ORDERS THAT CAN BE REPORTED ON >10	____
8	REPORTING HOURS FOR HOLIDAYS, ILLNESS, ETC.	____
9	HOURS SPENT ON MAINTENANCE WO'S VERSUS OTHERS (HOLIDAYS ETC.) REPORT	____
10	EMPLOYEE PAY RATES—REGULAR, OVERTIME, HOLIDAY	____

SECTION VIII—DOCUMENTATION

PACKAGE
RATING

1	SYSTEM OVERVIEW	____
2	OVERVIEW PER MODULE (MANUAL SUMMARY)	____
3	USERS MANUALS: FUNCTIONAL DESCRIPTION OF THE MODULES	____
4	USERS MANUALS: REQUIRED SCREENS OR PROGRAMS AND SEQUENCE	____

```
 5  USERS MANUALS: INPUT SCREENS                                            _____
 6  USERS MANUALS: EXPLANATION OF THE SCREENS                               _____
 7  USERS MANUALS: ERROR MESSAGE EXPLANATION                                _____
 8  USERS TRAINING MANUALS: FOR CLASSROOM PURPOSES                          _____
 9  USERS TRAINING MANUALS: WITH PREDEFINED SAMPLE (MANUAL & DATABASE)      _____
10  SYSTEM OUTLINE PER MODULE (INPUT/OUTPUT/FILES/PROCESS)                  _____
11  DESCRIPTION OF DATE ELEMENTS (USE IN PROGRAMS, VALUES, SOURCE OF DATA)  _____
12  INSTALLATION MANUAL INTERFACING OTHER SYSTEMS                           _____
13  INSTALLATION MANUAL: PARAMETER QUESTIONNAIRE                            _____
14  PROGRAMMERS MAINTENANCE MANUAL: PROGRAM LOGIC                           _____
15  PROGRAMMERS MAINTENANCE MANUAL: OUTPUT DESCRIPTION                      _____
16  PROGRAMMERS MAINTENANCE MANUAL: FILE SPECIFICATION                      _____
17  OPERATORS MANUAL                                                        _____
```

SECTION IX—HARDWARE PLATFORMS

PACKAGE
RATING

```
 1  MICRO VERSION AVAILABLE                                                 _____
 2  MINI VERSION AVAILABLE                                                  _____
 3  MAINFRAME VERSION AVAILABLE                                             _____
 4  PC/MINI/MAINFRAME VERSION COMPATIBILITY                                 _____
 5  MICRO/MAINFRAME LINK                                                    _____
 6  MINI/MAINFRAME TO PC EXTRACTION                                         _____
 7  PC TO MINI/MAINFRAME FILES TRANSFER                                     _____
 8  MULTI-USER SYSTEM                                                       _____
 9  PREPACKAGE SYSTEM                                                       _____
10  BUILDING BLOCKS (MODULES) FOR CUSTOM SETUP                             _____
11  HARDWARE SUPPLIER(S)                                                    _____
12  HARDWARE TYPES AND MODELS                                               _____
```

SECTION X—SYSTEM REQUIREMENTS

PACKAGE
RATING

```
 1  SYSTEM ACCEPTS INPUT FROM OTHER DATA SETS                               _____
 2  SYSTEM CAN INTERFACE WITH AN ACCOUNTS PAYABLE SYSTEM                    _____
 3  SYSTEM CAN INTERFACE WITH A PERSONNEL INFORMATION SYSTEM                _____
 4  SYSTEM CAN INTERFACE WITH A PURCHASING SYSTEM                           _____
 5  SYSTEM CAN INTERFACE WITH A CONDITION-MONITORING SYSTEM                 _____
 6  SYSTEM CAN INTERFACE WITH AN EXPERT SYSTEM                              _____
 7  GENERATES FREE FORMAT DATA SETS                                         _____
 8  OPTIONAL EXECUTIVE INFORMATION SYSTEM INTERFACE                         _____
```

PACKAGE
RATING

```
 1  TYPE OF DATABASE MANAGEMENT SYSTEM (DB2/VSAM/ORACLE)                    _____
 2  SQL APPLIED IN THE SYSTEM                                               _____
 3  SQL ADDITIONAL AVAILABLE                                                _____
 4  PROGRAMMING LANGUAGES                                                   _____
 5  REPORT GENERATOR AVAILABLE                                              _____
 6  GRAPHICS CAPABILITY SUPPORTED                                           _____
 7  SCREENS MULTI-LANGUAGES SUPPORTED, MULTI-CURRENCY                       _____
 8  ERROR MESSAGE FILES MULTI-LANGUAGES SUPPORTED                           _____
 9  BACKUP AND RECOVERY                                                     _____
10  TRANSACTION SECURITY                                                    _____
11  DATABASE FILED AUTHORIZATION                                            _____
12  FILED VALUE AUTHORIZATION                                               _____
13  MENU DRIVEN                                                             _____
14  MENU DRIVEN OPTIONAL USE (ACCESS TO SCREENS DIRECTLY)                   _____
15  ON-LINE HELP FACILITY IN ALL FUNCTIONS                                  _____
16  CURSOR ERROR CONTROL (FIELD BY FIELD EDIT)                              _____
17  FULL SCREEN ''FILLING THE BLANKS''                                      _____
18  DATA ENTRY BY BATCH INPUT                                               _____
19  DATA ENTRY BY ON-LINE INPUT                                             _____
20  PROGRAMMING SOURCE CODE STANDARD INCLUDED                               _____
21  PROGRAMMING SOURCE CODE ADDITIONAL AVAILABLE                            _____
```

22   USER EXITS AVAILABLE   _____
23   RESPONSE TIME FOR REAL TIME INPUT PROCESSING <4 SECONDS   _____
24   ON-LINE FIELD EXPLANATION BY CURSOR CONTROL   _____
25   GRAPHIC USER INTERFACE AVAILABLE (WINDOWS)   _____

                                                  PACKAGE
                                                  RATING

 1   >1000 WORK ORDERS IN ONE SYSTEM (PLANNED, ACTUAL, AND HISTORY)
 2   >10,000 WORK ORDERS IN ONE SYSTEM (PLANNED, ACTUAL, AND HISTORY)   _____
 3   >50,000 WORK ORDERS IN ONE SYSTEM (PLANNED, ACTUAL, AND HISTORY)   _____
 4   >1000 EQUIPMENTS IN ONE SYSTEM   _____
 5   >10,000 EQUIPMENTS IN ONE SYSTEM   _____
 6   >50 ACTIVITIES WITHIN A WORK ORDER   _____
 7   >100 ACTIVITIES WITHIN A WORK ORDER   _____
 8   >50 RESOURCES/GROUPS   _____
 9   >100 RESOURCES/GROUPS   _____
10   >200 STANDARD ROUTINGS AND/OR TASKS   _____
11   >100,000 SPARE PARTS SKUs   _____

                                                  PACKAGE
                                                  RATING

1   YEARS IN CMMS BUSINESS
2   NUMBER OF USER SITES   _____
3   NUMBER OF SITES IN THIS INDUSTRY   _____
4   CAN PROVIDE REFERENCE SITE VISITS   _____
5   TRAINING AND SUPPORT CAPABILITIES   _____
6   NUMBER OF RELEASES OVER PAST THREE YEARS   _____
7   ACTIVE USER GROUP   _____

Appendix C
Maintenance Terminology

acceptable condition	that condition agreed for a particular use, not less than that demanded by statutory requirements; meeting a functional standard for equipment operation
adjustments	minor tune-up actions requiring only hand tools, no parts, and usually lasting less than a half hour
apprentice	a tradesperson in training
area maintenance	a type of maintenance organization in which the first-line maintenance foreperson is responsible for all maintenance crafts within a certain area
assets	the physical resources of a business, such as plant, facilities, fleets, or their parts and components
asset list	a register of items usually with information on manufacturer, vendor, specifications, classification, costs, warranty, and tax status

asset management	the systematic planning and control of a physical resource throughout its economic life
asset number	a unique alphanumerical identification of an asset list, which is used for its management
availability	the period of scheduled time for which an asset is capable of performing its specified function, expressed as a percentage
backlog	work orders planned and prioritized, awaiting scheduling and execution
bar code	symbols for encoding data using lines of varying thickness, designating alphanumeric characters
bill of materials (BOM)	list of components and parts for an asset, usually structured in hierarchical layers from gross assemblies to minor items
breakdown	failure to perform to a functional standard
breakdown maintenance	a policy where no maintenance is done unless and until an item no longer meets its functional standard
CBM	see condition-based maintenance
changeout	remove a component or part and replace it with a new or rebuilt one
clean	to remove all sources of dirt, debris, and contamination for the purpose of inspection and to avoid chronic losses
CMMS	computerized maintenance management system
code	symbolic designation, used for identification
component	a constituent part of an asset, usually modular and replaceable, that is serialized and interchangeable

component number	designation, usually structured by system, group, or serial number
computer, mainframe	a digital calculator with the highest capacity and capability
computer, micro	moderate capability relative to a mini or mainframe
computer, mini	significant capacity, but less than a mainframe
computer, workstation	intermediate to a micro and mini computer
condition-based maintenance	maintenance based on the measured condition of an asset
coordination	daily adjustment of maintenance activities to achieve the best short-term use of resources or to accommodate changes in needs for service
corrective	maintenance done to bring an asset back to its standard functional performance
costs, life-cycle	the total cost of an item throughout its life including design, manufacture, operation, maintenance, and disposal
defect	a condition that causes deviation from design or expected performance
deferred maintenance	maintenance that can be or has been postponed from a schedule
deterioration rate	the rate at which an item approaches a departure from its functional standard
down	out of service, usually due to breakdown, unsatisfactory condition, or production scheduling

downtime	the period of time during which an item is not in a condition to perform its intended function
emergency	a condition requiring immediate corrective action for safety, environmental, or economic risk, caused by equipment breakdown
engineering work order (EWO)	a control document from engineering authorizing changes or modifications to a previous design or configuration
equipment configuration	list of assets usually arranged to simulate the process, or functional or sequential flow
equipment repair history	a chronological list of defaults, repairs, and costs on key assets so that chronic problems can be identified and corrected, and economic decisions made
equipment use	accumulated hours, cycles, distance, throughput, etc., of performance
examination	a comprehensive inspection with measurement and physical testing to determine the condition of an item
expert system	decision support software with some ability to make or evaluate decisions based on rules or experience parameters incorporated in the database
failure	termination of the ability of an item to perform its required function to a standard
failure analysis	a study of failures; to analyze the root causes, develop improvements, eliminate or reduce the occurrence of failures

failure coding	indexing the causes of equipment failure on which corrective action can be based, for example, lack of lubrication, operator abuse, material fatigue, etc.
fault tree analysis	a review of failures, faults, defects, and shortcomings based on a hierarchy or relationship to find the root cause
FMECA	failure mode, effect, and criticality analysis, a logical, progressive method used to understand the root causes of failures and their subsequent effect on production, safety, cost, quality, etc.
forecasting	the projection of the most probable: as in forecasting failures and maintenance activities
functional maintenance structure	a type of maintenance organization where the first-line maintenance foreperson is responsible for conducting a specific kind of maintenance, for example, pump maintenance, HVAC maintenance, etc.
hard time maintenance	periodic preventive maintenance based on calendar time
inspection	a review to determine maintenance needs and priority on equipment
inventory control	managing the acquisition, receipt, storing and issuance of materials and spare parts; managing the investment efficiency of the stores inventory
inventory turnover	ratio of the value of materials and parts issues annually to the value of materials and parts on-hand, expressed as percentage
issues	stock consumed through stores

labor availability	percentage of time that the maintenance crew is free to perform productive work during a scheduled working period
labor utilization	percentage of time that the maintenance crew is engaged in productive work during a scheduled working period
level of service (stores)	usually measured as the ratio of stockouts to total stores issues
logistics engineering	a systems engineering concept developed for military weapons systems; it advocates maintenance considerations in all phases of an equipment program to achieve specified reliability, maintainability, and availability requirements
maintainability	the rapidity and ease with which maintenance operations can be performed to help prevent malfunctions or correct them if they occur, usually measured as mean time to repair
maintenance	any activity carried out to retain an item in, or restore it to, an acceptable condition for use or to meet its functional standard
maintenance engineering	a staff function intended to ensure that maintenance techniques are effective, equipment is designed for optimum maintainability, persistent and chronic problems are analyzed, and corrective actions or modifications are made
maintenance policy	a principle guiding decisions for maintenance management
maintenance schedule	a comprehensive list of planned maintenance and its sequence of occurrence based on priority in a designated period of time

maintenance shut-down	a period of time during which a plant, department, process, or asset is removed from service specifically for maintenance
maintenance task routing file	a computer file containing skills, hours, and descriptions to perform standard maintenance tasks
menu	a selection of functional options in a software display
MTBF (mean time between failures)	see reliability
MTTR (mean time to repair)	see maintainability
NDT	non-destructive testing of equipment to detect abnormalities in physical, chemical or electrical characteristics, using such technologies as ultrasonics (thickness), liquid dye penetrants (cracks), x-ray (weld discontinuities), and voltage generators (resistance).
nonroutine maintenance	maintenance performed at irregular intervals, with each job unique, and based on inspection, failure, or condition
on-line	the state of being available and accessible while the CMMS is operating
outage	a term used in some industries, for example, electrical power distribution, to denote when an item or system is not in use
overhaul	a comprehensive examination and restoration of an item to an acceptable condition

periodic maintenance	cyclic maintenance actions carried out at regular intervals, based on repair history data, use or elapsed time
pick list	a selection of required stores items for a work order or task
planned maintenance	maintenance carried out according to a documented plan of tasks, skills, and resources
PM	see preventive maintenance
predictive maintenance	use of measured physical parameters against known engineering limits for detecting, analyzing, and correcting equipment problems before a failure occurs; examples include vibration analysis, sonic testing, dye testing, infrared testing, thermal testing, coolant analysis, tribology, and equipment history analysis
preventive maintenance (PM)	maintenance carried out at predetermined intervals, or to other prescribed criteria, and intended to reduce the likelihood of a functional failure
priority	the relative importance of a single job in relationship to other jobs, operational needs, safety, etc., and the time within which the job should be done; used for scheduling work orders
proactive	a style of initiative that is anticipatory and planned for
RCM	see reliability centered maintenance
rebuild	restore an item to an acceptable condition in accordance with the original design specifications

reliability	the ability of an item to perform a required function under stated conditions for a stated period of time; is usually expressed as the mean time between failures
reliability analysis	the process of identifying maintenance of significant items and classifying them with respect to malfunction on safety, environmental, operational, and economic consequences. Possible failure mode of an item is identified and an appropriate maintenance policy is assigned to counter it. Subsets are failure mode, effect, and criticality analysis (FMECA), fault tree analysis (FTA), risk analysis, and HAZOP analysis.
reliability centered maintenance	optimizing maintenance intervention and tactics to meet predetermined reliability goals
repair	to restore an item to an acceptable condition by the renewal, replacement, or mending of worn or damaged parts
rotable	components that are rebuilt after their useful life and rotated through maintenance stores back to use
running maintenance	maintenance that can be done while the asset is in service
schedule compliance	the number of scheduled jobs actually accomplished during the period covered by an approved schedule; also the number of scheduled labor hours actually worked against a planned number of scheduled labor hours, expressed as percentage

scheduled discard	replacement of an item at a fixed, predetermined interval, regardless of its current condition
scheduled maintenance	any maintenance that is planned and prioritized to be done at a predetermined time
scoping	outlining the extent and detail of work to be done and the resources needed
servicing	the replenishment of consumables needed to keep an item in operating condition
shelf life	that period of time during which materials in storage remain in an acceptable condition
shutdown	that period of time when equipment is out of service
shutdown maintenance	maintenance done while the asset is out of service, as in the annual plant shutdown
specifications	physical, chemical, or performance characteristics of equipment, parts, or work required to meet minimum acceptable standards
standby	assets installed or available but not in use
standing work order	a work order that remains open, usually for the annual budget cycle, to accommodate information on small jobs or for specific tasks
terotechnology	an integration of management, financial, engineering, operating maintenance, and other practices applied to physical assets in pursuit of an economical life cycle

total productive maintenance	companywide equipment management program emphasizing operator involvement in equipment maintenance and continuous improvement in equipment effectiveness
tradesperson	skilled craft workers who normally have completed an apprenticeship program
unplanned maintenance	maintenance done without planning or scheduling; could be related to a breakdown, running repair, or corrective work
up	in a condition suitable for use
utilization factor	use or availability
variance analysis	interpretation of the causes for a difference between actual and some norm, budget, or estimate
work order (WO)	a unique control document that comprehensively describes the job to be done; may include formal requisition for maintenance, authorization, and charge codes, as well as what actually was done
work request	a simple request for maintenance service or work requiring no planning or scheduling but usually a statement of the problem
workload	the number of labor hours needed to carry out a maintenance program, including all scheduled and unscheduled work and maintenance support of project work

About the Author

John Campbell is the Partner-in-Charge of Coopers & Lybrand's international Centre of Excellence for Maintenance Management located in Toronto, Canada. He is a graduate in Metallurgical Engineering and Materials Science from the University of Toronto and, prior to joining Coopers & Lybrand, had held various plant engineering and management positions in the manufacturing and processing industry.

He is a frequent speaker on maintenance management issues and has consulted for clients in a variety of international settings.

Index

Books from Productivity, Inc.

Productivity, Inc. publishes books that empower individuals and companies to achieve excellence in quality, productivity, and the creative involvement of all employees. Through steadfast efforts to support the vision and strategy of continuous improvement, Productivity, Inc. delivers today's leading-edge tools and techniques gathered directly from industry leaders around the world. Call toll-free (800) 394-6868 for our free catalog.

The 5S System:
Workplace Organization and Standardization (video)
Tel-A-Train and the Productivity Development Team

5S is a method front-line workers can really use to improve workplace safety, reduce waste, simplify work processes, improve equipment maintenance and troubleshooting, and ensure product quality. It's the basis for any on-the-floor improvement activity. Now, using learn-while-doing training techniques, workshop teams can follow this step-by-step video training at their own pace, and implement 5S in their won target area. This complete video training program introduces you to each of the 5S activities and its rationale, and powerfully leads your team through implementation.
Includes seven video tapes, facilitator's guide, and participant's guide.
$1,995.00 / Order 5SV7-B231
Introductory tape only / $495.00 / Order 5SV1-B231

Beyond Corporate Transformation
A Whole Systems Approach to Creating and Sustaining High Performance
Christopher W. Head

When do your employees resist change? They resist change when they don't understand the changes that are taking place, they see little or no perceived benefit of doing things differently, or they do not feel involved. Which is why employees who will be affected by a transformation must effect the changes. Realizing that anything short of total employee involvement in the change process jeopardizes success, this book emphasizes that it is the responsibility of every employee to act as a change agent. Learn how to go beyond piece meal incremental changes, beyond reengineering, beyond the limited idea of change to encompass a whole systems approach to creating and sustaining a competitive advantage. Through a revolutionary, integrated, employee-oriented leadership philosophy, this book illustrates how to transform an organization by tapping into the full potential of every employee.
ISBN 1-56327-176-1 / 240 pages / $35.00 / Order BEYOND-B231

Productivity, Inc., Dept. BK, P.O. Box 13390, Portland, OR 97213-0390
Telephone: 1-800-394-6868   Fax: 1-800-394-6286

Becoming Lean
Inside Stories of U.S. Manufacturers
Jeffrey Liker

Most other books on lean management focus on technical methods and offer a picture of what a lean system should look like. Some provide snapshots of before and after. This is the first book to provide technical descriptions of successful solutions and performance improvements. The first book to include powerful first-hand accounts of the complete process of change, its impact on the entire organization, and the rewards and benefits of becoming lean. At the heart of this book you will find the stories of American manufacturers who have successfully implemented lean methods. Authors offer personalized accounts of their organization's lean transformation, including struggles and successes, frustrations and surprises. Now you have a unique opportunity to go inside their implementation process to see what worked, what didn't, and why. Many of these executives and managers who led the charge to becoming lean in their organizations tell their stories here for the first time!
ISBN 1-56327-173-7 / 350 pages / $35.00 / Order LEAN-B231

Implementing a Lean Management System
Thomas L. Jackson with Karen R. Jones

Does your company think and act ahead of technological change, ahead of the customer, and ahead of the competition? Thinking strategically requires a company to face these questions with a clear future image of itself. *Implementing a Lean Management System* lays out a comprehensive management system for aligning the firm's vision of the future with market realities. Based on hoshin management, the Japanese strategic planning method used by top managers for driving TQM throughout an organization, Lean Man-agement is about deploying vision, strategy, and policy to all levels of daily activity. It is an eminently practical methodology emerging out of the implementation of continuous improvement methods and employee involvement. The key tools of this book build on multiskilling, the knowledge of the worker, and an understanding of the role of the new lean manufacturer.
ISBN 1-56327-085-4 / 182 pages / $65.00 / Order ILMS-B231

TO ORDER: Write, phone, or fax Productivity, Inc., Dept. BK, P.O. Box 13390, Portland, OR 97213-0390, phone 1-800-394-6868, fax 1-800-394-6286. Outside the U.S. phone (503) 235-0600; fax (503) 235-0909. Send check or charge to your credit card (American Express, Visa, MasterCard accepted).

U.S. ORDERS: Add $5 shipping for first book, $2 each additional for UPS surface delivery. Add $5 for each AV program containing 1 or 2 tapes; add $15 for each AV program containing 3 or more tapes. We offer attractive quantity discounts for bulk purchases of individual or mixed titles; call for more information.

ORDER BY E-MAIL: Order 24 hours a day from anywhere in the world. Use either address:
   To order: **info@productivityinc.com**
   To view the online catalog and/or order: **http://www.productivityinc.com/**

QUANTITY DISCOUNTS: For information on quantity discounts, please contact our sales department.

INTERNATIONAL ORDERS: Write, phone, or fax for quote and indicate shipping method desired. For international callers, the telephone number is 503-235-0600 and the fax number is 503-235-0909. Prepayment in U.S. dollars must accompany your order (checks must be drawn on U.S. banks). When quote is returned with payment, your order will be shipped promptly by the method requested.

NOTE: Prices are in U.S. dollars and are subject to change without notice.

Productivity, Inc., Dept. BK, P.O. Box 13390, Portland, OR 97213-0390
Telephone: 1-800-394-6868   Fax: 1-800-394-6286

ABOUT THE SHOPFLOOR SERIES

Put powerful and proven improvement tools in the hands of your entire workforce! Progressive shopfloor improvement techniques are imperative for manufacturers who want to stay competitive and to achieve world class excellence. And it's the comprehensive education of all shopfloor workers that ensures full participation and success when implementing new programs. The Shopfloor Series books make practical information accessible to everyone by presenting major concepts and tools in simple, clear language and at a reading level that has been adjusted for operators by skilled instructional designers. One main idea is presented every two to four pages so that the book can be picked up and put down easily. Each chapter begins with an overview and ends with a summary section. Helpful illustrations are used throughout.

Books currently in the Shopfloor Series include:

5S for Operators
5 Pillars of the Visual Workplace
The Productivity Development Team
ISBN 1-56327-123-0 / 133 pages
Order 5SOP-B231 / $25.00

Quick Changeover for Operators
The SMED System
The Productivity Development Team
ISBN 1-56327-125-7 / 93 pages
Order QCOOP-B231 / $25.00

Mistake-Proofing for Operators
The Productivity Development Team
ISBN 1-56327-127-3 / 93 pages
Order ZQCOP-B231 / $25.00

Just-In-Time for Operators
The Productivity Development Team
ISBN 1-56327-133-8 / 84 pages
Order JITOP-B231 / $25.00

TPM for Supervisors
The Productivity Development Team
ISBN 1-56327-161-3 / 96 pages
Order TPMSUP-B231 / $25.00

TPM Team Guide
Kunio Shirose
ISBN 1-56327-079-X / 175 pages
Order TGUIDE-B231 / $25.00

Autonomous Maintenance
Japan Institute of Plant Maintenance
ISBN 1-56327-082-X / 138 pages
Order AUTMOP-B231 / $25.00

Focused Equipment Improvement for TPM Teams
Japan Institute of Plant Maintenance
ISBN 1-56327-081-1 / 138 pages
Order FEIOP-B231 / $25.00

TPM for Every Operator
Japan Institute of Plant Maintenance
ISBN 1-56327-080-3 / 136 pages
Order TPMEO-B231 / $25.00

OEE for Operators
Overall Equipment Effectiveness
The Productivity Development Team
ISBN 1-56327-221-0 / 96 pages
Order OEEOP-B231 / $25.00

Cellular Manufacturing
The Productivity Development Team
ISBN 1-56327-213-X / 96 pages
Order CELLP-B231 / $25.00

Productivity, Inc., Dept. BK, P.O. Box 13390, Portland, OR 97213-0390
Telephone: 1-800-394-6868   Fax: 1-800-394-6286

Productivity, Inc. Consulting, Training, Workshops, and Conferences
EDUCATION...IMPLEMENTATION...RESULTS

Productivity, Inc. is the leading American consulting, training, and publishing company focusing on delivering improvement technology to the global manufacturing industry.

Productivity, Inc. prides itself on delivering today's leading performance improvement tools and methodologies to enhance rapid, ongoing, measurable results. Whether you need assistance with long-term planning or focused, results-driven training, Productivity, Inc.'s world-class consultants can enhance your pursuit of competitive advantage. In concert with your management team, Productivity, Inc. will focus on implementing the principles of Value-Adding Management, Total Quality Management, Just-in-Time, and Total Productive Maintenance. Each approach is supported by Productivity's wide array of team-based tools: Standardization, One-Piece Flow, Hoshin Planning, Quick Changeover, Mistake-Proofing, Kanban, Problem Solving with CEDAC, Visual Workplace, Visual Office, Autonomous Maintenance, Overall Equipment Effectiveness, Design of Experiments, Quality Function Deployment, Ergonomics, and more! And, based on continuing research, Productivity, Inc. expands its offering every year.

Productivity, Inc.'s conferences provide an excellent opportunity to interact with the best of the best. Each year our national conferences bring together the leading practitioners of world-class, high-performance strategies. Our workshops, forums, plant tours, and master series are scheduled throughout the U.S. to provide the opportunity for continuous improvement in key areas of lean management and production.

Productivity, Inc. is known for significant improvement on the shop floor and the bottom line. Through years of repeat business, an expanding and loyal client base continues to recommend Productivity, Inc. to their colleagues. Contact Productivity, Inc. to learn how we can tailor our services to fit your needs.